Education, Movement
and the Curriculum

Education, Movement and the Curriculum

Peter J. Arnold

 The Falmer Press

(A member of the Taylor & Francis Group)
New York ● Philadelphia ● London

UK   The Falmer Press, Falmer House, Barcombe, Lewes, East Sussex, BN8 5DL

USA   The Falmer Press, Taylor & Francis Inc., 242 Cherry Street, Philadelphia, PA 19106-1906

© 1988 P. J. Arnold

First published 1988

Library of Congress Cataloging in Publication Data is available on request

ISBN 1 85000 412 9
ISBN 1 85000 413 7 (pbk.)

Jacket design by Caroline Archer

Typeset in 11/13 Bembo by
Imago Publishing Ltd, Thame, Oxon

Printed in Great Britain by Taylor & Francis (Printers) Ltd, Basingstoke

Contents

Dedicated to

Jane, Louise and Clare

Preface and Acknowledgements

The themes comprising this book derive in the main from lectures given to physical education students as a part of their professional preparation to become teachers. The purpose of the lecture course, which perhaps is even more needed today, was to get students to think clearly about what place physical activities had in the curriculum and on what grounds, if at all, they could be justified. Most students came to see that being clear about *what* and *why* one was trying to do not only helped with practical decision-making when planning lessons, but in the formulation of a coherent argument about the worth of their subject when they came to leave college and join departments of dance or physical education in schools. Few would disagree that the demand for accountability (and the ability to provide a rationale for a course) in the foreseeable future will continue. It is hoped that *Education, Movement and the Curriculum* will provide assistance not only in these necessary endeavours but in the provision of a more extended notion of 'professionality' than is sometimes the case.

A great many issues arose out of the course, as a result of giving papers and seminar discussion, and I am grateful to several generations of students for the help they have given me in the clarification of my own thoughts as a result of their difficulties, perceptive observations and questions.

I am also indebted to a number of colleagues who were good enough to read and make comment upon, one or more of the chapters when they were in draft form. In this respect I would like to thank in particular Christine Macintyre and Phyllis Early for making a number of useful suggestions. In addition I would like to thank Eddie Still, the Lothian Region Senior Physical Education Adviser, for scrutinizing, in a meticulous way, the last three chapters, as a result of which a number of improvements were made.

Education, Movement and the Curriculum

Several chapters of the book are revised or modified versions of previously published articles and I would like to thank the following journals for permission to use much of this material for inclusion in this volume: *The Journal of Aesthetic Education; Journal of Moral Education; Journal of the Philosophy of Education; Journal of the Philosophy of Sport; Physical Education Review;* and *Quest.*

My thanks also go to the library staff at Dunfermline College (now a part of Moray House College) for their unfailing help in tracking down and obtaining, when asked, books and articles from other institutions.

Needless to say, despite the generous assistance afforded me, I am responsible for any errors that remain.

Peter J Arnold
March 1988

viii

Introduction

Over the past three or four decades a great deal has been done to establish the philosophy of education not only as a legitimate field of study in its own right but as an important element in the professional preparation of teachers. Despite this, however, few colleges or universities concerned with 'physical education', or what I prefer to call 'movement', provide what are philosophically adequate or appropriate courses for young teachers to embark upon a career in this branch of education. This book sets out to fill this gap.

Although in recent years there has been a growing interest in courses to do with the 'philosophy of sport' these, somewhat like many of those in 'sports psychology' or 'sports sociology', make little or no attempt in a deliberate and structured way to relate them to current educational issues and concerns. In the past there have been some authors who have recognized the importance of this task (Arnold, 1979b; Davis, 1961; Harper *et al* 1977; Shea, 1978; Zeigler, 1964 and 1978), but none has performed it in the manner that is envisaged here. Rather they have laid the parameters of what is necessary, or pointed up the possibilities of an 'isms'[1] approach, or tackled one aspect of what is required but none has undertaken the detailed analytic work necessary to uphold or sustain a particular and justifiable position. The purpose of this book is to attempt this job. The aim then of *Education, Movement and the Curriculum* is to philosophically explore the relationship between the concept education and the concept movement and to see what implications this has for the teacher and for curriculum planning and its evaluation. The intention is that it will not only provide a sound basis for taught courses and discussion about the place of movement activities in the context of school life but be of practical use when it comes to making decisions about what, how and why something should be taught. Content, process and justification are all part and parcel of a philosophic approach to educational problems.

But what it may be asked is the philosophy of education? What does it see its task to be? Broadly speaking it can be said that the philosophy of education draws on the established branches of philosophy such as epistemology, ethics, aesthetics and the philosophy of mind, and brings them together in ways which are relevant to education issues. 'It is just philosophy' as Langford (1968) has put it, 'but with an eye to the practices and problems of those engaged in or concerned with education; just as the psychology of education is simply those parts of psychology which are relevant to education' (p.14) Above all the philosophy of education is concerned with the meaning of education and how what is implied or advocated by the term can be justified. The nature and purpose of education is, of course, a perennial and thorny one and cannot easily be disassociated from prevailing societal values and ideologies. Nonetheless, few people in the liberal West would wish to question the view that school-based education should help promote the development of the individual as a person through the activities of learning and teaching. Even, however, if this broad outline of the 'meaning' of education is accepted it begs further questions such as: How is this best done? What sort of development is being referred to? What are the methods that should be adopted? Clearly any adequate concept of education will at least provide guideline answers to these and similar questions. Peters (1966) in his analysis of education provides criteria which it is maintained are implicit in central cases of 'education' (p.45). In their abbreviated form they are:

(i) that education implies the transmission of what is worthwhile ...;

(ii) that 'education' must involve knowledge and understanding ...;

(iii) That 'education' at least rules out some procedures of transmission, on the grounds that they lack wittingness and voluntariness on the part of the learner.

In general the criteria of education provided by Peters seem helpful and relatively straightforward. Individual development is surely centrally to do with the transmission of knowledge and understanding. The question that arises, however is what sort of knowledge and understanding is being referred to here? As will be seen in chapter 2 it is possible to interpret knowledge in a narrowly intellectualistic sense. On the other hand it can be broadened to include a practical know-

2

ledge of how to do or perform physical activities successfully and to certain standards. Surely too, Peters is right in characterizing education as much in terms of the type of procedures adopted as in what should be taught. What is of importance here is that only morally acceptable procedures are considered as appropriate to education. Other procedures, which are often done in the name of education, such as drilling, training, conditioning and indoctrination are unacceptable largely because they are limiting, or immoral in the sense they do not accord the learner with the respect that he is due. It is precisely this respect of one person for another that should form a constituent part of all educative situations. This point, particularly as it relates to sport and the manner in which it is taught and learnt, is an important one. It will be pursued extensively in chapters 3, 4 and 5 which respectively are to do with the development of character, the meaning of sportsmanship and the problem of competition. The central purpose of these topics is to clarify some of the issues and see how and to what extent, if at all, they can be reconciled with the concept of education. No book, as far as I know, has previously attempted this. It will be noted that although references used are drawn mainly from British and American literature, the questions raised are universal in nature.

A particular point arising from Peters' characterization of education should be brought out. It is that the activities pursued should have intrinsic value and be pursued for their own sake rather than for some reason external to them. This point will be explicated in the first chapter on 'aims and objectives', developed further in all succeeding chapters, including those (6 and 7) on sport and dance in relation to the aesthetic and aesthetic education, and specifically articulated in terms of the movement curriculum and its evaluation in chapters 8, 9 and 10. What should be made clear is that for the purposes of this book, partially in order to narrow its scope and partially to enable me to modify and extend what can be described as the 'knowledge cum ethical' view of education, I am taking education to mean an initiation of pupils into those worthwhile pursuits of an 'academic' and 'physical' kind for their own sake and in a morally defensible manner.

It will be appreciated that although education is (or should be) the main function of the school the terms 'education' and 'schooling' are by no means synonymous. Schooling has a broader connotation than education, especially when the latter is used, as above, in its evaluative rather than descriptive sense. The school then is importantly concerned with education but not confined to it. It is also concerned and involved with other necessary and/or desirable aspects of life and upbringing such as health, vocational training and preparation for civic responsibility. What is being emphasized here is that schooling is concerned with more things, and for good reason, than just education. Education is not, and cannot be, the sole criterion for what should be taught in schools. There is often justification in teaching things for good instrumental reasons as well as for reasons of intrinsic value. This point is of key importance and should be borne in mind when the objectives of the movement curriculum come to be discussed for it will help make clear the difference between the objectives of movement as a form of education and other objectives of the movement curriculum which form a legitimate part of schooling. It should be noted that this book, whilst highlighting the difference between the one and the other, will be concerned only with an explication of the former.

If it can be accepted that education approximates to what has been outlined it follows that movement, as an aspect of education must fall, if coherence and consistency are to be preserved, within its broad parameters. But what more specifically is movement? And how does it or should it relate to education? It should be made clear if misunderstanding is to be avoided that it is not to be mistaken for or confused with what, first in Great Britain and then in the United States, has become known as 'movement education', which is derived largely from the effort qualities and movement themes originally developed by Rudolf Laban (1963) and which have since been systematized into a teaching approach by workers like Morrison (1969) and North (1973) and more recently by Logsdon and Barrett and their colleagues (1984). Rather, the concept of movement as I propose using the term was first explicated by the present writer in 1973 (Arnold, 1973) and which has received several updatings since then (Arnold, 1979 and 1980). Chapter 8 should be seen as a further modification. What is distinctive about the concept of movement is that it has three differentiable but interrelated dimensions — 'about', 'through' and 'in'. Briefly put, movement relates to education, schooling, and the curriculum in the following three ways. The first dimension of 'about' movement is concerned with the development of disciplinary-based knowledge and understanding of physical activities because this is seen in itself of interest and value. The second dimension of 'through' movement is concerned with the instrumental use of physical activities in the promotion of educational objectives other than its own (for example, learning of mathematics) as well as for other desirable purposes. The third dimension of 'in' movement is concerned with initiating pupils into that culturally valued family of physical pursuits (which for convenience in terms of the school curriculum are collectively called Movement), so that they come to 'know how' to successfully participate in them, care for them and enjoy them for what they are. What it is important to note about this Three Dimensional Model of the Movement Curriculum, as I shall call it, is that its conceptual framework is such that it permits both the educative elements of movement (dimensions one and three) and the desirable, if utilitarian purposes of schooling, such as fitness, socialization and preparation for wholesome use of leisure time (dimension two), to be planned without the ambiguities, difficulties and confusions that characterize many other curriculum models. One great advantage of the Three Dimensional Model of the Movement Curriculum, is that it recognizes and separates out the difference between the intrinsic and extrinsic reasons for doing something. By doing so it overcomes the ambivalence and contradiction with which the term 'physical education' is often associated.

Note

1   Reference here is made to such major orientations as naturalization, idealism, realism, pragmatism, and existentialism. See, for example, Zeigler (1964 and 1978).

1   Education: Values, Aims and Objectives

The aim of this book is to explore and clarify the relationship between education and the study, practice and use of that family of physical activities comprised of games, swimming, dance, athletics, gymnastics, outdoor pursuits and so on which I shall collectively refer to as 'movement'.[1]

In order to provide a perspective for what follows this first chapter will make as clear as possible what stance towards education is being adopted and how the question of values, aims and objectives relate to it.

Descriptive and Evaluative Senses of Education

Education can be understood in one of two main senses — descriptively or evaluatively. A descriptive account of education is an attempt to report *how things are* as an actual state of affairs without any judgments of value necessarily being made. Thus it is possible to describe education as 'the process by which the individual acquires the many physical and social capacities demanded of him by the group into which he is born and within which he must function' (Anderson, *et al*, 1968, pp.12–15). An evaluative account of education on the other hand is one which sets out in an attempt to assess and render judgments about *how things ought to be* rather than as they are. It should be made clear that in what follows attention will be confined to this second or evaluative account. Implicit then in education is a concern for what is valuable.

Education and Values

One way of trying to see how education and values are related is to ask the question 'Which value or values are most appropriate to being educated?' A further question might be 'Which value or values are of most worth?'

When confronted with such fundamentally important questions it is not unusual for philosophers[2] to look to such values as:

(i)   happiness and its pursuit;
(ii)   knowledge and its acquisition;
(iii) moral virtue and its development;
(iv)   self-realization and its furtherance.

Theories abound as to how these values relate to one another and which one of them if at all is superior to the others. Are knowledge and moral virtue for example subordinate to happiness? Is it possible to maintain that all these values can be regarded as ends without the necessity to make the choice about which of them is to reign supreme?

It is the stance adopted towards such values that largely determines our view about what should be undertaken in the name of education. Concepts of education are invariably value-laden and reflect a particular view about what is worthwhile and what should be done in schools. Because of this they are *prescriptive*. They imply if not overtly state what the content and methods ought to be if education is to result.[3]

Before returning to say something more about education in relation to these values, it would be helpful, if misunderstanding is to be avoided later, to distinguish between intrinsic and extrinsic values.

Intrinsic and Instrumental Values of Education

In discussions about education the question arises as to whether education is valuable in itself or whether it is only valuable in so far as it serves some instrumental purpose beyond that which is done. To put the matter another way 'Is education good as an end in itself or only good as a means of serving other ends outside itself?'

Let the second possibility be taken first. If education were only good as a means of serving ends outside itself its results or *consequences* would only be 'good' 'bad' or 'neutral' according to the nature of the ends in view. Education, if seen merely as a tool to fulfil ends extrinsic to itself, might equally well serve virtually any end assigned to it whether it be to do with vocational training, citizenship, indust-rial production, guerilla warfare, political indoctrination, racial pre-judice, or the cultivation or skills required by a Marquis de Sade. In each of these cases it would be possible to move in the direction of fulfilling the chosen purpose by selecting appropriate subject matter and by adapting methods which it is thought would bring about what was intended in the most efficient way possible.

Movement, like other subjects, can be used for political, social or economic ends. Huxley (1969, pp.187–8) in his book *Ends and Means* understands this clearly. In writing of sport, for example, he observes:

> Like every other instrument that man has invented, sport can be used for good or evil purposes. Used well, it can teach endurance and encourage a sense of fair play and a respect for rules, co-ordinated effort and the subordination of personal interests to those of the group. Used badly it can encourage personal vanity and group vanity, greedy desire for victory and hatred for rivals, an intolerant esprit de corps and con-tempt for people who are beyond a certain arbitrarily selected role.

He continues:

> Sport can be either a preparation for war or, in some measure, a substitute for war; a trainer either of potential war-mongers or of potential peace-lovers; an educative influence forming either militarists or men who will be ready and able to apply the principles of pacifism in every activity of life.

If education were conceived in this purely 'functional' way it might be regarded as simply a means and be lacking in any particular content of its own or any distinctive procedures that were in themselves valu-able. Education as an evaluative concept would therefore have to be abandoned.

Ends and means in education, however, do not have to be looked at in this instrumental way. Instead, it is possible to regard education as having its own 'ends' and 'means' both of which are considered intrinsically valuable and integral to the educative process upon which a person is engaged. Both Dewey (1916) and Peters (1963) are insistent that education should not be regarded as primarily an instrumentality for the attainment of some external aim or end. Rather they hold that education, both as a concept and as activity, is value laden and directed. Although for Dewey (1916, pp.89–90) education is pre-dominantly concerned with the 'reconstruction or reorganization of experience which adds to the meaning of experience, and which increases ability to direct the course of subsequent experience' and for Peters (1966) education is centrally concerned with knowledge and understanding, both are agreed that what is done with regard to content and procedure should be intrinsically valuable. Whereas Dewey (1916, p.109) asserts that 'no study or discipline is educative unless it is worthwhile in its own immediate having' and Peters (1963, pp.144–6) speaks of 'worthwhile activities' which are valuable in themselves, each is clear that education is not worthy of the name if it is reduced to a means which serves ends outside itself.

What is being maintained is that education is (or should be) comprised of intrinsically valuable activities and procedures. This in effect means that what is sometimes referred to as subject matter and method both becomes ends and that the latter is not seen merely as a means of promoting the former. Education as an evaluative concept in other words is concerned no less with the *manner* of the doing than with the content or *what* is done. It will be seen that there is no disjunction between ends and means in education because means, or intrinsically valuable procedures are as much ends as the activities selected. It should be noted that for both Dewey (1916) and Peters (1981b) there is a close relationship between the processes of education and the nature of democracy.

What emerges from this discussion of ends and means in relation to educational values is this: that the values of education are concerned with the promotion of intrinsically worthwhile activities as well as intrinsically worthwhile procedures. Both *content* and *procedures* are the ends and aims of education. Together they form a mode of life that has its own integrity.

Education: Aims, Objectives and Outcomes

As has been suggested the question of values in education raises the question of aims. It is in what is valued and in what order of priority that determine aims. Values, it can be said, give authorization and content to aims. They provide the reference point by which judgments are made with regard to what has been achieved. Educational aims are often spoken about in two main ways:

(i)   they are often spoken of in relation to ends which are considered desirable;

(ii) they are often spoken of also in relation to contexts (for example, the classroom or gymnasium) in which it is thought important to get people (teachers, students) to specify more clearly what they are trying to do.

Aims in general then are useful in so far as they give direction in terms of concentration and effort towards goals that are not too palpable or close to hand. Aims also suggest, as Peters (1973, p. 14) points out, the possibility of failure or falling short in some way.

In education *objectives* should be seen as being logically related to aims. They can be regarded as so many relevant staging posts on the way towards the realization of an aim. Objectives in relation to aims are more immediate, more specific, more tangible and more achieveable. They are concerned with the practicalization of aims.

The chief function of objectives in the words of Taba (1962) is 'to guide the making of curriculum decisions on what to cover, what to emphasize, what content to select, and which learning experiences to stress' (p. 197).

Objectives in education are perhaps best seen as intermediate targets towards achieving intrinsically desirable ends. They should normally be realistic and result in progressive steps towards effective learning. If soccer, for example, is seen as a 'worthwhile activity', then its constituent skills will become necessary objectives in the teaching of it.

The term *outcome* refers to the effect or consequences of a particular form of learning or teaching. An outcome may or may not be in keeping with what was intended. With good teaching what is set as a learning objective will coincide with what results. When a stated objective is achieved the consequence is an *intended outcome*. There are occasions, however, when a particular outcome may not coincide with the objective set. An *unintended outcome* is something which arises or results from learning but which may not be in accord with the stated objective. Unintended outcomes can either be good or bad. They can either help or hinder learning; have a positive or negative effect. The teaching of a particular game strategy, for example, may lead fortuitously to a sense of cameraderie or a regrettable outbreak of anti-social behavior.

In 'physical education', as is sometimes the case with other subjects, there is a good deal of confusion in understanding the relationship between aims, objectives and outcomes. In the Schools' Council Enquiry[4] (see table below) into physical education, for example, which was set up to discover details for current practices with a view to improving future curriculum development, it was learnt that there was a considerable difference between what teachers considered to be *objectives* and what they thought to be the most important *outcomes* of their work. The table, shown below, reveals something of the problem.

What is of particular interest is the failure to make any meaningful distinction between such broad aims (or values) as 'self-realization', for example; and more specified forms of behaviour such as 'motor skills'. Even in the case of 'motor skills', however, it is necessary to be clear about *which* motor skills are worth cultivating. Just to acquire 'motor skills' without reference to 'context' or 'purpose' tells us little. What is referred to is left too vague. In the absence of context and purpose there is little chance of providing a justification for them being taught at all. The question also arises as to whether many of the items listed for example, 'emotional stability' and 'social competence', are any more the concern of movement than of other subjects such as drama or music. Can it be shown, even on instrumental grounds, that physical activities are any more effective as a means of bringing about these 'objectives' than others? In any case should such objectives be considered as appropriate objectives for education or should they be classed as beneficial but fortuitous outcomes?

Again even if objectives like 'moral development' or aesthetic appreciation' can be shown to relate logically to such movement activities as 'sport' and 'dance' does it follow that this is equally so for movement activities in general? The answer to this question is surely

Table 1 Objectives of the PE Programme (Found in the literature and ranked according to teachers views)

Rank for Men		Rank for Women
6	Emotional stability	3
3	Self-realization	2
1st	Leisure time pursuits	4
7	Social competence	6
5	Moral development	5
4	Organic development	8
2	Motor skills	1st
9	Aesthetic appreciation	9
8	Cognitive development	7
Most Important Effects On Pupils As Judged By Teachers In Order Of Importance		
(a)	Social awareness and responsibility	
(b)	General physical development	
(c)	Self-awareness	
(d)	General motor ability	
(e)	General interest in school	
(f)	Cognitive judgment	

'no'. This is not the case and cannot reasonably be expected. Whereas it can be said, for example, that aesthetic objectives are appropriate in dance because dance is inherently concerned with the aesthetic, the same cannot be said of rugby. The point to be understood is that movement, like other subjects in the school curriculum, must state with more validity and precision what its objectives are and show how these arise from and relate to those individual activities that collectively comprise it. Only when this task has been accomplished can the distinctive and comprehensive nature of the contribution of movement to education begin. It is one of the prime jobs of philosophical analysis to assist in this endeavour. It may, on the face of it, appear a modest role but in fact it is of critical importance for if it is not done with care and justification the whole basis for the inclusion of movement in the curriculum is left in a quagmire of undifferentiated claims and unverifiable contentions. The chapters that follow this one may be regarded as making a start in this direction.

Education as Initiation

In returning to the question of values in relation to education it has become common among philosophers in the analytic tradition to criticize such ultimate concerns as 'happiness' or 'self-realization' as being very helpful to school-based education on two main grounds. Firstly, they are considered largely vague and indeterminate notions and in consequence offer little clear guidance about what activities should be pursued or what procedures adopted. Secondly, even if some sort of programme could be agreed upon it would mainly be judged on its utilitarian value and not because of its intrinsic worth. One account of education which overcomes the criticisms raised about accepting such values as 'happiness' or 'self-realization' as a basis for education is that which I shall refer to as the 'initiation' view. This has been formulated predominantly by the combined writings of P H Hirst and R S Peters (1970). The values which are the heart of their analysis of education are those of knowledge and morality. They are seen, especially perhaps during the formative years, as being more appropriate, as well as being more tangible entities with which to deal. Furthermore it is the intrinsic worth of these values that is upheld and it is the instantiation of them in *what* is done and *how* it is done that is at the centre of what is regarded as education. In short they argue that education is concerned with the transmission of what is worthwhile in a way which is morally acceptable. Peters (1966) has various criteria for attempting to establish what is 'worthwhile' but briefly put what is worthwhile may be associated with knowledge in the form of intellectual pursuits on account of (a) their wide ranging cognitive content; and (b) their ability to contribute to the quality of living.[5] 'The overall aim of education', he suggests (1981b, p.81) 'is to get children *on the inside* of the activities and forms of awareness characterizing what we would call a civilized form of life'. *Instrumental values*, unless they are directly concerned with the promotion of what is intrinsically worthwhile, are not the concern of education. Hence to see activities in terms of such extrinsic considerations as improving industrial efficiency or vocational training is to misunderstand the nature of education. Such concerns are not the aims of education even though, as will be made clear later, they may form a useful part of what the school does. Even so education, when pursued for its own sake, may and almost assuredly will, produce *outcomes* that are of use to the furtherance of these concerns. Indeed as Bailey (1984, p.29) points out, in providing pupils with the intrinsic worth of knowledge and understanding, they are at the same time necessarily being provided with that which 'has the most general relevance and utility for anything they are likely to want to do'.

The initiation view of education is a powerfully argued and important account of education. It insists on the intrinsic worth of certain activities and on the manner in which they should be taught, regardless of the use to which they may be subsequently put. It is within this general evaluative framework that the case for the place of movement in education will proceed. It will be seen at the outset, however, that the greatest problem for movement on the orthodox rendering of the initiation view is its narrowly intellectualistic approach to knowledge. A discussion and proposed solution to this problem will be the subject of the next chapter.

Notes

1   I prefer the term Movement to Physical Education not only because of the dualism implicitly condoned in the latter term (i.e. 'physical' as opposed to 'mental' education) but also because as a concept it permits us to go, if necessary, beyond education, a term to which 'physical education' is (or should be) logically tied.
2   For further reading on these values or theories of 'goodness' see Hospers (1967, pp.580–95). See also his *Human Conduct* (1985).
3   Two recent books that support the general point being made here are by Bigge (1982) and Ozman and Craver (1981). For a good discussion on

educational aims in a democratic society see Peters (1963, pp.32–50) and Dewey (1916). For an up to date summary on the relationship between aims, values and education see Garforth (1985).

4   See Kane (1976, pp.78 and 90).
5   For a questioning of whether or not 'intrinsic aims' are the only valid ones for education consult White (1982).

2   Education, Practical Knowledge and Movement

It was said at the end of the last chapter that the initiation view of education is concerned with the acquisition of knowledge of an itellectual kind in a morally acceptable manner. Put another way, it is seen as the development of mind which is brought about by an initiation of the young into those public traditions which are enshrined in 'the language concepts, beliefs and rules of a society' (Peters, 1966, p.49)[1]. In particular it is concerned with those 'forms of knowledge' which have been progressively differentiated over the centuries and which now number 'some seven or eight distinguishable cognitive structures, each of which involves the making of a distinctive form of reasoned judgment and is, therefore, a unique expression of man's rationality' (Hirst, 1974, p.25). In terms of the curriculum what is being referred to here are those theoretically orientated academic or intellectual pursuits which have become known as religion, ethics, history, mathematics, aesthetics, science — natural and social, and philosophy, each of which, it is maintained, is autonomous or logically separate from the others in that it has (a) its own set of distinctive concepts; and (b) its own way of testing whether a claim is true or false.

The concepts, for example, of gravity, atom, neuron, are characteristic of the physical sciences, just as harmony, expression and style belong to aesthetics; or God, sin and predestination are part of religious terminology. Again, whereas in science certain forms of experimental technique are required involving measurement and observation, in history it is more a question of meticulously cross-checking between a matrix of clues and connections from a variety of sources to try and bring about an accurate interpretation of events which is always subject to the check of others.

It is important to note that the type of knowledge with which the initiation view of education is concerned is predominantly theoretical, rather than practical. It is directed to what can be known and said about the world rather than acting intelligently in it. Hirst (*ibid*) for example, writes:

> The domain of knowledge I take to be centrally the domain of true propositions or statements, and the question of their being logically distinct forms of knowledge to be the question of their being logically distinct types of true propositions or statements. (p.85)

That the development of mind is associated with such intellectual pursuits as science, history and literary appreciation is abundantly evident. 'No matter what the ability of the child may be' maintains Hirst (*ibid*), 'The heart of all his development as a rational being is ... intellectual, and we must never lose sight of these ends on which so much else, nearly everything else, depends' (p.28). Given this stance about knowledge in relation to education it is not surprising that these differentiated structures or different ways of thinking about the world are prescribed as 'universal objectives' for the curriculum. If these basic 'forms of knowledge' are denied, it is argued, then rationality itself is denied, for it is only by being initiated into them that we are able to make sense of our experience.

A summary of the main features of the argument is given below.

(i)   Education is about the development of mind.

(ii) 'Mind' is logically determined by 'knowledge', and 'to ac- quire knowledge ... is to have mind in a fuller sense'.

(iii) Knowledge lies in the structuring of experience by concepts and the accompanying criteria of objectivity (in applying those concepts, making inferences, etc).

(iv) In so far as there are (a) logically different kinds of concepts; (b) different criteria of objectivity; (c) distinctive methods for further structuring experience, knowledge is differenti- ated into (seven) fundamentally distinct forms. These are: mathematics, physical sciences, morals, aesthetics, religion, knowledge of our own and other people's minds (human sciences, history), philosophy.

(v)   The formal characteristics of each kind of knowledge must (logically) be respected in the articulation of curriculum objectives, i.e. a scheme of education principally governed by the distinctions between the various forms of knowledge.

It should be understood that what Peters designates as 'worthwhile' or 'serious' in educational terms are those activities which have:

(a) wide ranging cognitive content; and
(b) are able to illuminate other areas of life and contribute much to the quality of living (Peters, 1966, p.159).

By way of contrast, games, it is maintained, have little cognitive content for: 'There is very little to know about riding bicycles, swimming or golf. It is largely a matter of "knowing how" rather than of "knowing that", of knack rather than understanding'. Peters continues: 'Furthermore what there is to know (about games) throws very little light on much else' (*ibid*). In contrast to intellectual pursuits, which have been associated with the development of rationality, games are neither 'serious' nor 'worthwhile'. Two points emerge from Peters' analysis of games in relation to education. The first is that games (and by implication other physical activities) are not inherently concerned with what constitutes the nature of an educational activity; that in fact, like play, they are 'set apart from the main business of living'(*ibid*). The second point is that if games are used or manipulated in some way in order to link them artificially with 'serious' or 'intellectual' pursuits, games will lose whatever integrity they have.

The most that Peters is able to concede about the importance of 'physical education' (somewhat a misnomer in this context) is that a lack of fitness may impair the possibility of a rational life. 'Without a fit body' he says 'a man's attempts to answer the question "why do this rather than that?" might be sluggish or slovenly' (*ibid*, p.163).

A Critique of the Initiation View of Education

Perhaps enough has been said about the initiation view of education and its reference to physical activities to express some observations about it. Clearly much of what it upholds is of fundamental importance to our knowledge and understanding of the world and, of course, few people would wish to deny this. Nonetheless, in its pure form, it must be seen as a limited and impoverished form of education. There are at least four main criticisms that can be made. The first criticism is that it sees education *only* in terms of the development of mind rather than in terms of what it is to be a whole person with capacities to do as well as to think. A corollary of this preoccupation with mind reflects an unacknowledged but nonetheless implicit dualism: an acceptance of the logical separation of mind from body and a priority of place being given to the former in the educational scheme of things. Peters (*ibid*, p.211), for example, comments that 'People only begin to think of themselves as persons, as centres of valuation, decision and choice, insofar as the fact that consciousness is individuated into distinct centres, *linked* with distinct physical bodies'. A second criticism, even if one accepts this hidden metaphysic of the person, which seems to impregnate much of what is written, the term 'mind' is used in a narrowly intellectualistic way. It overemphasizes a certain view of the 'cognitive' and associates it with the type of knowledge and understanding that is of a propositional kind. It is taken up, in other words, with knowledge of a theoretical kind rather than of a practical kind; of 'knowing that' such and such is the case, for example, 'a parallelogram is a four sided figure, the opposite sides of which are parallel and equal', rather than 'knowing how' to do something, for example, play hockey. There is little appreciation of the fact 'the cognitive' enters into practical pursuits and that it is not an exclusive preserve of intellectual pursuits. 'Knowing how', in any case, is not, as Peters suggests, 'just a matter of knack, rather than understanding'. To characterize it as such is to misunderstand its distinctive character or significance in human affairs[2].

A third criticism is that because what is 'worthwhile' in the curriculum is centred upon the seven 'forms of knowledge' which are largely, if not exclusively of a propositional kind, it results in an academically prescribed education which contains little by way of practical education[3]. Practical pursuits in fact are seen of value only in so far as they can assist in the development of intellectual understanding. Such a view of knowledge and education is reductionist in nature for what it amounts to is the denial that practical pursuits, including such physical activities as swimming, dance and games, as well as others, such as pottery, arts and craft, cookery, woodwork and metalwork, have sufficient about them that makes them worthwhile. The fact that such pursuits as sport and dance in our culture are central elements in our way of life and are a source of interest and value to many people, is disregarded. If these or other practical activities are to find a place in the 'serious' curriculum at all it can only be, the argument goes, on grounds of how they can assist in the acquisition of academic knowledge.

A fourth general criticism of the initiation view of education, and one which grows out of the ones just made, is that it does not develop 'the whole person'. By concentrating upon the cognitive-intellectual aspects of education it neglects other aspects of what it is to be a person which remain important if a full and more complete form of education is to be achieved. Apart from that realm of practical pursuits, which have been mentioned, it distorts and misrepresents several of those areas which are held to be central to any programme of education. In such modes of discourse, for example, as aesthetics and morality, it is clear that the language and concepts of those modes should be understood but what is not apparent is that taste or sensitivity be cultivated, or that kindness, sympathy and tolerance towards others developed. Crudely put, it can be said, that in these modes the critical faculties are put at a premium whilst such qualities as imagination, feeling, virtue and will are neglected or undervalued[4]. Martin (1981) in portraying the type of person such a view of education is likely to produce writes:

> The received theory's liberally educated person will be taught to see the world through the lenses of the seven forms of knowledge, if seven there be, but not to act in the world. Nor will that person be encouraged to acquire feelings and emotions. The theory's liberally educated person will be provided with knowledge about others, but will not be taught to care about their welfare, let alone act kindly towards them. That person will be given some understanding of society, but will not be taught to feel its injustices or even to be concerned over its fate. The received theory conceives of a liberally educated person as an ivory tower person: one who can reason, but has no desire to solve problems in the real world; one who understands science, but does no worry about the uses to which it is put; one who grasps the concepts of biology, but is not disposed to exercise or eat wisely; one who can reach flawless moral conclusions, but has neither the sensitivity nor the skill to carry them out effectively.

All in all the initiation view of education as it is prescribed by Hirst and Peters presents a distorted picture of human nature and the curriculum it advocates does less than justice to the full range of valued human achievements.

Needless to say some educationists like Pring (1976) and Reid (1961) have argued against such a reductionist view of knowledge and education, especially when set against the variety of human accomplishments and the different ways there are of knowing. Bantock (1971) in perceiving the inappropriateness of this form of education for the academically least able suggested an alternative form of education which gives greater prominence to the concrete, the practical and the 'affective and artistic' in education. Even the current attention towards promoting technical and vocational skills and personal and social development may be seen as a reaction against an academic type of education for all, especially when many pupils are unsuited to it and/or disenchanted by it.

An elaboration of these points, however, will not be embarked upon here. Perhaps enough has been said to indicate some to the more obvious inadequacies of the initiation view of education, especially as a prescription for every person.

The purpose of the remaining part of this chapter is to make the point that practical knowledge or 'knowing how' is different from propositional knowledge or 'knowing that' but no less important when it comes to the education of the whole person.

The Rationality of Practical Knowledge and Knowing How

It is well recognized by philosophers that apart from theoretical or propositional knowledge or the knowledge of 'knowing that' something is the case, which is the kind of knowledge with which Hirst's 'forms of knowledge' is concerned, there is another kind of knowledge which is practical and is concerned with 'knowing how' to do, or proceed with, certain kinds of activities. Whereas propositional knowledge is concerned with substantiating such statements as 'I know that the Battle of Hastings was in 1066'; 'I know that metals when heated expand'; 'I know that the opposite angles of a parallelogram are equal', as being true; practical knowledge is concerned with certain forms of performative competence such as when I say 'I know how to drive a car'; 'I know how to make a book shelf'; or 'I know how to play tennis'.

What is important to understand about these two types of knowledge is that each has its own rationality. 'The main difference between theoretical and practical knowledge' writes Carr, 'is that whereas the concern of the former is with the discovery of truths that are adequately supported by reason and confirmed by experience, the latter is concerned with the execution of purpose in action, conducted in a rational manner and confirmed by a reasonable degree of success'(1981, p.60).

Although it was Aristotle (1973, p.28) who originally pointed out the distinction between theoretical and practical reasoning it was left to Ryle (1949, pp.26–60) to underline the point that both 'knowing that' and 'knowing how' are expressions of human rationality. He argued that whereas 'knowing-that' is a function of human theorizing 'knowing-how' is an expression of rational practice. The one, he maintained, cannot be reduced to the other. Anscombe (1957) also argues that whereas in theoretical reasoning we aim to move logically from statements about the world to conclusions about it, in practical reasoning we are directed towards the execution and realization of our intentions and purposes. The central point at stake here is that when a person 'knows how' to do, certain things of a particular sort (such as making a table or playing squash) his knowledge is actualized or exercised in what he does. His intelligence is made manifest in his deeds, skills and accomplishments.

A point made by Ryle and worth repeating here is that a practice is not as the 'intellectualist legend' suggests a step-child of theory. Often it is its precursor. That is to say some theories arise from the study of an already existing practice. It is not always necessary therefore first to do some theory before being able to practice something. This way round of things with activities such as crafts, art and sport is, I think, particularly so. If one wishes to teach a head spring or a tennis serve one teaches *how* to do these things directly. It is not logically necessary first to do a bit of theory and then do a bit of practice. This, of course, is not to say that theory cannot sometimes usefully inform and guide practice. What it does refute it that it is a precondition for knowing how to do something. This point poses serious difficulties for the 'forms of knowledge' view of education. In a domain such as aesthetics, for example, is one more concerned with teaching the activities of dance, music and mime and so on or with the theory *about* them? In any case what does it or what can it mean to say, for example, that aesthetics as a form of knowledge is to do with the making of true propositions and statements? Again, in the moral sphere is or should education be more concerned with getting children to behave in a morally responsible manner or with getting them to understand and use the language of moral discourse? Surely, although in each of these areas there is a close relationship between the practice of certain activities and the appropriate forms of conceptual development that go with them, it is the practice of painting, singing or games or the practice of morality in terms of responsible conduct that should be the prime concern of the educator.

Knowing How and Physical Activities

It has been suggested that practical reasoning or knowing how is essentially concerned with taking action or bringing things about in the world, rather than with the construction of theories and the establishing of what is propositionally true. It has also been suggested that 'knowing how' and 'knowing that' are different yet fundamentally important expressions of human rationality and should therefore feature in any well-rounded programme of education. In order to be clear about what is being referred to when we speak of 'knowing how' in relation to physical activities it is necessary to develop its understanding further. It will be helpful firstly to distinguish between 'knowing how' in a *weak* sense and 'knowing how' in a *strong* sense. Whereas the weak sense refers to a person who is physically able to do something, for example, a cartwheel, and can show or demonstrate that he is able to do it but when asked how he did it has little or nothing to say by way of description or understanding, the strong sense refers to a person who is not able to do what he says he can do but when asked how he does it, is able to provide, with insight and understanding, a descriptive account of how it was done. In the weak sense reference is not being made to a person who was able to do something by accident or as a fluke, but to person who did what he did *intentionally* and is able to repeat it at will but simply has no apparent grasp of how he did it in the sense of being able to provide any sort of coherent account of the steps or procedures he took to do what he did. He knows how in the sense that he is able but not in the sense of being able to articulate what he did. Ask the brilliant, instinctive but inarticulate goalkeeper how he saved the goal he might say 'like this' and show how rather than say how.

Many actions in sport, I think, are of this sort. A child many be able to 'pick up' the basic skills of soccer but is not conscious of the means or procedures by which he comes to acquire them. As Curtis (1977) observes: '"knowing how" in the sense of being able to do it and knowing how to do it in the sense of being able to say how it is done are often very different affairs' (p.84). Even within the framework of a game a player may implicitly be following certain rule-governed procedures but is unable to say what those procedures are.

In contrast to this weak sense, 'knowing how' in the strong sense is characterized by the person not only *intentionally* being able to do or perform actions successfully but by being able to *identify* and *give an account* of how they were done. He will, if asked, be able to make explicit the rule-governed procedures by which he did what he is able to do. His understanding of what he is doing or has done will be based upon a well understood grasp of how he does what he is able to do. He will be able to state how means relate to ends. What will mark out knowing how in this strong sense is that the person will not only be able to do something successfully but be able to give an intelligible account of how it is done. In this strong sense intentionally being able to do something is not a sufficient condition for knowing how.

Further explication of the strong sense of knowing how requires at least two additional comments to be made:

1   *Knowing how involves rule-following procedures*

The strong sense of knowing how then involves an understanding of the rule-following procedures and an account of how something is done. What is done *implicity* must in ordinary discourse be capable of being rendered *explicitly*. To know how in this strong sense is to understand the nature, purpose and context of a particular action that is undertaken. To play a game, for example, involves having a know-ledge and understanding of the rules of the game so that play proceeds within this understood framework. The player will understand what he is permitted and not permitted to do. What is provided by a statement of the rules in effect, however, is a *procedural rationale* for how to take part in *that* game. Put another way what a statement of the rules of a game provide is not a *theoretical* statement but a *descriptive* statement about how to proceed. If one wishes to practise football successfully it is necessary to understand and follow the rules which both characterize and govern it.

2   *Skills as acquired contextual abilities*

Skills, it can be said, are exemplifications of practical reasoning in terms of knowing how to do something competently to certain mini-mum standards. Unlike habits they involve the agent intelligently monitoring what he is doing whilst he is doing it, together with an ability to adjust to changing circumstances when this is required. Whereas a habitual performer tends to stick to relatively fixed and patterned routines in a relatively unthinking way, the skilful perfor-mer will be thinking and appraising what to do next if the task or purpose is to be achieved as effectively as is possible for him. Whereas habits, relatively speaking, are static in their execution, skills are dynamic.

In the contexts of sport, for example, skill mastery is made manifest in the way something is tackled and brought about. The good golfer does not merely draw upon a stock of well drilled habits or conditioned movement patterns learned against a set of unchanging circumstances. Instead he intelligently takes account of the changed or changing circumstances in which he finds himself at a given moment. Wind, rain, different lies, and so on, make each round of golf different in some way from previous ones. Each stroke requires thought before it is played. The good golfer is able to select the right club with knowledge and understanding and play it reliably and accurately. He is not a *habitual* performer but an *intelligent* one. He is able to see what is required of a situation and is able to carry out what needs to be done successfully. Much of what is involved in order to produce a perfect round of golf is clearly depicted by Nicklaus (1974). He writes:

> First I would have to have achieved 100 per cent analytical objectivity — recognized the ideal shot for each situation. Second, having recognized the perfect shot, I would have to have resolved to play it — no compromises. Third, having re-cognized and resolved to play the perfect shot, I would have to have executed it perfectly — no technical hitches. (pp.253–4)

Similarly in a sport such as soccer where the contextual circumstances involve a moving ball as well as a dispositional fluidity of players, skilfulness, at the highest level, is not so much recognized by the ability to trap, dribble, head and lay-off the ball competently, though these skills remain important, as by an ability to utilize these acquired learnings intelligently as the game is being played. These separately acquired skills will only be of use if they serve in the development and promotion of tactical procedures and dynamic strategies. In soccer playing, as in other games, where there is an open and constantly changing environment, it is not simply a mastered set of appropriate basic skills that is required but their relevant and co-ordinated de-velopment in the game as it unfolds. The good soccer player will not only be a skilful player in the sense of having mastered certain basic competencies but will be able to perceive what needs to be done at a given moment and direct his energies and talents towards its achievement.

A Characterization of Knowing How

Perhaps enough has been said about the distinctive features of the rationality of practical knowledge or knowing how and their connec-tion with physical activities. The main points are summarized below.

Paractical knowledge, or 'knowing how', unlike propositional knowledge or 'knowing that', is centrally concerned with:

(i) *Practice* not *theory*; or at least not only theory
(ii) *Action*, not just or only *thought* or *belief*

(iii)   Intentionally *doing* something *in* the world rather than just *thinking* or providing information or speculating *about* the world.

In the context of movement, sport and physical education, any complete characterization of 'knowing how' would include the following points:

(i)   That it is *performative.*

(ii)   That it involves the power to understand and follow *rule-governed procedures.*

(iii) That it involves *intelligent critical action* i.e. the agent or performer is thinking (i.e. has the capacity to monitor and respond to what he is doing) whilst he is doing it.

(iv)   That it involves *standards* of minimal competence, i.e. knowing always involves knowing how to do something in particular (playing the piano, throwing the javelin) and this involves trying to get the activity 'right'.

In sum 'knowing how' is essentially concerned with the mastery of *skills* and *'being able to'* perform or participate in a given activity *successfully with understanding.*

Educational Implications

Having said something about the difference between 'theoretical knowledge' and 'practical knowing', or 'knowing that' and 'knowing how', and of the indispensability of the latter to all practical pursuits, including sport and games, it becomes necessary to ask what significance this has for education? The answer to this question is that it has immense significance not only in terms of what it is to be a person but in terms of human growth and development.[5] To enter fully into this discussion, however, would take me far from my prime concern. Nonetheless, some general points can be made. Firstly, if granted for the moment, that education is centrally to do with the acquisition of knowledge and the development of rationality it does seem in the interests of a balanced life that it should not be confined to the cultivation of *one* type of knowledge and *one* type of rationality. As has been pointed out there are at least two kinds of rationality: theoretical and practical. Each have different ends and each require different kinds of thinking to achieve these ends. The end of theoretical rationality is universal truth; the end of practical rationality is appropriate action. It would seem perfectly reasonable to suggest therefore that a 'liberal education' has as much to do with initiating the young into a society's valued practices as it is with initiating them into its theoretically constructed forms of thought. To conceive of knowledge and rationality only in terms of propositions *about* the world is to conceive of it in narrowly intellectualistic terms.

Secondly, if the sort of developmental impoverishment that has been pointed to, is to be avoided it would necessarily call for a greater attention and prominence being given to those activities which embrace the notion of agency and action rather than being restricted to those which are essentially concerned with reflection. It is here, of course, that such activities as games, swimming, dance, gymnastics, as well as painting, sculpturing, singing and instrumental playing, have a strong case for inclusion in any broadly based programme of education. It is clear that in addition to knowledge *that* such-and-such is the case (or is not the case), there is knowledge of *how* to successfully participate in various forms of practical pursuits, and in each case particular skills need to be learned. It is through practice and experience that performances become more accomplished and it is through the exemplification of public standards in relation to an activity that it is possible to say of a person: 'he knows how to do it'. The point being upheld here is that 'physical activities', no less than 'artistic activities', are important manifestations of a culture's practical life and, together with 'intellectual pursuits', should form a necessary part of what it is to be educated.

Thirdly, it seems clear that if education is to do with the enlargement and enrichment of awareness then the learning of skills has an important place in the development of a person regardless of the usefulness of the purposes to which they may be directed. Although skills are most frequently seen only in instrumental terms they can also have intrinsic interest and be cultivated for their own sake. A person who simply likes swimming, for example, may wish to improve his front crawl and take joy in the doing of it, regardless of what benefits it may bring in terms of such considerations as health, survival or winning races. It is always necessary therefore in an educational context especially to distinguish between the skilled performance of a person in terms of a contextual purpose to be fulfilled, and the *intrinsic satisfaction* it affords him. It is often the case, of course, that the one goes with the other, although this need not always be so. What is important from the point of view of the expansion of consciousness is that, in one sense at least, skills are never entirely 'closed' but are always 'open' to more discrete and subtle layers of consciousness not only in terms of their acquisition and mastery but of the performer's own identity in relation to them.[6] The fact that an activity or skill provides intrinsic satisfaction for the participant, of course, does not by itself make something educationally worthwhile; but when this is combined with a development of knowledge and understanding and a caring attitude towards what is accomplished by way of publically attested standards, then what is meant by an educational process is well on the way to being realized.

What emerges from this chapter is that education, even when seen as being centrally concerned with knowledge and rationality, goes far beyond a curriculum based upon theoretically constructed forms of propositional discourse. It is concerned also with an initiation into a whole range of practical pursuits such as sport and dance which form a significant and valued part of our culture. It is to a detailed consideration of these that attention will now be given.

Notes

1 The initiation view of education in schools is perhaps best understood as an introduction of pupils to the intellectual life of their society.
2 It should be acknowledged that Hirst's (1979, p.102) rendering of 'knowing how' in a more recent article is a good deal more sophisticated than this but he nonetheless gives the impression that practical activities, although containing elements of 'knowing that', are on the periphery of educational concerns and that what is of central importance is intellectual understanding.
3 For a well argued case against the initiation model of education and for the inclusion of practical pursuits in the curriculum consult Carr (1981). See also O'Hear (1981) and Schilling (1986).
4 For an elaboration on these points see Warnock (1977, pp.129–65).
5 For an article which touches upon this theme from the point of view of the process and ethic of self-actualization see Arnold (1979a).
6 For an elaboration on this point see Arnold (1979b), especially chapter 4.

3   Sport, Moral Education and the Development of Character

Despite a long and respected tradition, which goes back to Plato (1955), that there is an important relationship between a person's physical life and the development and formation of his character, it has been argued over the past few years that sport (and the playing of games) is of no moral consequence and that it is therefore a 'non-serious' or trivial affair. This position about sport (and games)[1], which is embodied in the writings of some advocates of the initiation approach to education, stems from the view that it is discontinuous with the 'business of life' and is therefore, when compared to life's concerns, morally unimportant and has no ethical value. It is in a word 'non-serious' rather than 'serious'. This, of course, is not to say that sport cannot be taken or played seriously. The basis of the claim that sport is 'non-serious' lies not in the approach or attitude of the players towards what they do but in the view that sport, because of its separatedness from life, is morally inconsequential. Such a view about sport, it will be argued, lies partially upon a misunderstood view of sport and partially upon a too ready assimilation of sport to the realm of play. It is this latter point that will be examined first and I will return to the former point later. It will be appreciated that both issues are of interest for they not only affect the way in which sport is conceived but more particularly, the position of movement (which is largely to do with sport and games) in the context of education and the place it occupies in the curriculum.

One of the most influential writers on play in recent years has been Huizinga (1970)[2]. It was he who gave credence to the view that play is separate from life when he spoke of it as being a 'free activity standing, quite consciously, outside "ordinary" life as being "not serious"' (p.32). Further, he expressed something of its 'self-contained' nature when he spoke of it as proceeding 'within its own proper boundaries of time and space according to its own fixed rules and in an orderly manner' (*ibid*). In keeping with the same point he suggested that 'the game depends upon the temporary acceptance by the players of a set of rules which "cut off" the activity within games from events in the "real" world . . .'. He adds: 'Play as a type of leisure activity . . . entails the temporary creation of a sphere of irreality' (*ibid*, p.33).

In the initiation view of education it is quite clear that writers like Dearden and Peters are considerably indebted to Huizinga. Dearden, (1968, pp.100–1) for example, in speaking of play as 'non-serious' characterizes it firstly as being 'self-contained' in the sense of being set apart from the duties, deliberations and developing projects which make up the web of purposes of ordinary life; and secondly, by referring to it as being 'immediate in its attractiveness', by which he seems to have in mind something like spontaneous absorption. In contrast to the 'non-serious' activity of play are those 'serious' activities which on the one hand are to do with a society's 'cultural values' — and here he cites the 'arts and sciences' (1969, p.85) as examples, and on the other hand, are those matters of 'basic interest' which are to do with private prudence and social morality (1968, p.97). It will be seen then that in contrast to the 'non-serious' activities of play, 'serious' activities are to do with knowledge and truth as well as with morality.[3] Play then for Dearden 'is a non-serious and self-contained activity which we engage in just for the satisfaction involved in it' (1969, p.84).

Peters (1966, chapter 5) too in his book *Ethics and Education*, adopts the distinction made by Huizinga and argues that curriculum activities can be divided into those which are 'serious' or worthwhile and those which are 'non-serious' and non-worthwhile. Into the category of the 'serious', it will be recalled, Peters (*ibid*, p.159) places such intellectual pursuits as science, history, literary appreciation and philosophy. In short it is apparent that he associates the serious with Hirst's (1974, pp.30–35 and pp.84–100) 'forms of knowledge' on account of them illuminating other areas of life and contributing to the quality of living; and having a wide-ranging cognitive content. It is these two factors which distinguished them from 'games'. What it is important to note here is that play and the 'non-serious' have come to be associated with sport and by implication physical education. That this transposition in Peters' thinking has taken place is quite clear. He writes:

Part of what is meant by calling something a game is that it is set apart from the main business of living, complete in itself, and limited to particular times and places. (1966, p.159)

Having designated games as being 'non-serious' he goes on:

> Games can be conceived of as being of educational significance and therefore serious only so far as they provide opportunities for acquiring knowledge qualities of mind and character, aesthetic grace and skills that have application in a wider area of life' (*ibid*).

What is of particular interest in the context of our present concern is that he acknowledges that:

> Their importance for moral education, for instance is obvious enough. For virtues such as courage, fairness, persistence, loyalty have to be exhibited in a pre-eminent degree in many games — especially those involving team work. Others give scope for judgment, coolheadedness, and insight into other people's motives. (*ibid*, pp.159–60)

He ends by saying that:

> The presumption of those who believe in the educational importance of games is that the situations which they present and in which virtues have to be cultivated and exercised, are relevantly similar to situations in life of a less self-contained character. (*ibid*, p.160)

The basis of Peters' position about games seems to be this: that although games, like 'serious' pursuits can be pursued for their own sake, they are not, unlike 'serious' pursuits, in and of themselves of moral concern. They can nonetheless be made to serve serious or educational purposes if they are looked upon and used in an instrumental fashion. If this comes about, however, so that they are regarded as 'exercises in morality', for example, 'they can cease to be merely games' (*ibid*, p.159). Cricket, observes Peters, is classed as a game because it is 'morally unimportant' (*ibid*, p.158).

What seems clear then is that in Peters' view, games in the form of sports, are 'non-serious' in that they are not directly or inherently concerned with our intellectual or moral lives. It is because I think the latter position in particular is wrong that I propose to examine the matter further. It will be argued that those games which are sports (hockey, rugby, soccer, etc.) are 'serious' in the sense that, far from being set apart from the moral sphere they are inextricably bound up with it.[4]

In arguing a case along these lines it is intended to uphold the view that sport is essentially an intrinsically moral practice and that when it is corrupted or demeaned in some way, as it is from time to time, it ceases to be sport in any full sense of that term. When this occurs it stops being all that it can and should be. In this respect it is not unlike the concept of education which, when it falls short of promoting knowledge and understanding in a morally acceptable way, should no longer be called education. In sport, as in education, it will be suggested, there are ethical considerations involved which are integral to its successful practice.

In attempting to draw out the relationship between sport and morality it is proposed firstly, to say something about morality and moral education before going on to look at the practice of sport as fairness and the development and formation of character in sport.

Morality and Moral Education

In broad terms it can be said that morality is concerned with our relations with others. It involves our consideration and concern for others as well as for ourselves. It is interested in how to distinguish 'right' from 'wrong' and 'good' from 'bad'. Morality is therefore involved with values and a consideration of principles to which reference can be made before entering into an activity or engaging upon a particular course of action. Such principles as universality or impartiality, rational benevolence and liberty are frequently pointed to as underpinning the character of moral discourse and action. Universality implies that the principles identified must be applicable to all. Rational benevolence recognizes the importance of reason giving as well as recognizing the interests of all so that no individual or group is wittingly favoured at the expense of another. Liberty brings attention to the fact that for an act to be a moral act it must be a free act. That is to say it is a freely chosen act and one for which the agent can be held responsible and accountable.

The term moral education refers to the intentional bringing about of moral growth. It is according to Kohlberg (1971, p.25) the encouragement of a capacity for moral judgment. More than this it is also concerned with a disposition to act in accordance with whatever moral judgments are made. What marks out moral education is that it is a deliberate and intentional activity which is concerned with the cultivation of principled moral judgment and a willing disposition to act upon it. Both rational autonomy and strength of will are involved here. To be able to form a moral judgment and yet not act upon it is to fall short of what moral education entails. It is when a moral judgment is translated into an appropriate moral action that moral conduct and therefore moral education is mostly clearly expressed. McIntosh (1979) clearly has something similar in mind when he writes:

> the morally educated person is expected not only to be able to make moral judgments but act upon them. The moral life necessitates a host of personal dispositions. The moral person must think the issue through to the limits of his capacity but if morally right action is to occur the person must be disposed to act on his moral judgment. (p.167)

What differentiates 'moral education' from 'moral training', which implies a form of drilling in getting pupils to conform to moral rules without much understanding of moral principles, is that the pupils themselves are encouraged to think critically on moral issues in the light of fundamental moral principles and that they make their own rational judgments which they translate into appropriate moral action. An important criterion of success in moral education, writes Meakin (1982):

> is the degree to which an individual is willing and able to subject a given set of moral rules to his or her own critical scrutiny and decide in the light of reason whether to act on these or on some self-chosen set of rules. (p.65)

It might be thought, from what has been said, that it is always necessary first to think and then to act but this is not necessarily the case. What happens quite often in practice, and perhaps especially in sport, is that the player acts spontaneously, as is often the case in acts of sportsmanship, without reasoning out first why he acted in the way that he did. What is important here is that a morally educated person is able to display his moral concern without necessarily having to reason out his course of action in advance. This, however, does not mean that if challenged he could not justify what he did by pointing to the underlying moral rules and principles by which all actions can be judged. In this respect no distinction holds between those actions that take place within the framework of games and sports and those that do not.

Aspin (1975) underlines much of what I shall be maintaining when he observes:

> Morality therefore, and a *fortiori* moral education is concerned with helping us to understand that human life is beset with

obligations of one sort and another. One of its aims will thus be to give us a knowledge of the rules which function in this particular 'game' and to seek to develop in us a grasp of its underlying principles, together with the ability to apply these rules intelligently and to have the settled disposition to do so. (p.57)

It should not be thought in view of what has been said that moral education is only concerned with the making of moral judgments and having the will and capacity to act upon them. Clearly other considerations are also important. Wilson *et al* (1967), for example, in addition to the cognitive, and volitional aspects of moral education also recognize that the affective dimension has its part to play. To enable children to see that the feelings of other people count as much as their own, and an ability to empathize with other people in various sorts of situations, are as much a part of being morally educated as being able to think and to act in a principled way. Pring (1984, p.117), in seeing moral education as a part of personal and social development, advocates a form of curriculum which takes account of at least four factors. First, *cognitive capacity*, which includes the developing capacity to think in terms of fairness and in terms of principles. Second, *the facts to be known*, which, in the case of sport, would involve knowing the rules. Third, a bundle of interrelated considerations, which he labels *attitudes, feelings and dispositions*. This would include, in the case of sport the generation of an appropriate attitude towards the rules and the referee, as well as a respect for and empathy towards one's fellow players. Fourth, *practical application*. This, again in the case of sport, involves the concrete living out of the previous three factors. To do this takes 'strength of character', especially if what is seen to be 'right', goes against prevailing group pressure.

Kant (1960), in his reflections on education recognized that there is more to education than book learning. He believed strongly that the essential thing about education is the formation of the person by his own efforts in terms of his talents and his character (1960, pp.2–3). For him the commandment to live in accordance with nature paves the way for the commandment to go beyond nature by the exercise of reason in terms of duty and law (*ibid*, p.108). For Kant the primary end of education is the development of moral character. If this is to be achieved each pupil must not only be accorded respect by others by seeing him as an end and never merely as a means but by the cultivation of self-respect. When a child (or person) lies he degrades himself by robbing himself of the dignity and trust that every person should have (*ibid*, p.102). Lying, cheating and other forms of taking advantage of another are not only to be regretted in social terms but also in terms of the moral damage it does to his own character. It will be argued shortly that such self-demanding acts are as applicable in the sphere of sport and games no less than in other spheres of life for, like other activities, they are both social and personal in nature. Lying and cheating are to be condemned just as much as honesty and fair play are to be upheld for they affect the self-respect of the person just as they affect the quality of relations with others. Kant did not see the formation of character as something happening overnight but rather as something that emerges from a constant and prolonged process of self-formation. It is marked by a steadfast pursuit of purpose based upon reasoned and universalizable moral principles. It should be noted that Peter's (1981a, p.29) depiction of 'having character', which emphasizes the regulation of conduct in accordance with high order principles, is very much in keeping with this last point. What in general should be understood is that the notion of character in its moral sense, as Wright (1971, p.203) observes, cannot be defined 'through an inventory of actions performed, as by a description of the principles that give coherence, and meaning to an individual's behaviour, and of the relatively enduring dispositions that underly it'.

Kant's views on the relationship between education and the formation of character are important to movement in at least three respects. Firstly, it is seen as a moral one based upon reasoned and universalizable principles. Secondly, it emphasizes the giving of respect to others as well as having respect for oneself. Thirdly it draws attention to the fact that the development of character is not a passive process but an autonomously active and purposeful one to do with self-formation. All these points I shall want to uphold when it comes to sport and conduct appropriate to it. Before tackling this task more specifically, however, it will be helpful to look at the ethical basis of sport which will be depicted as a distinctive form of practice concerned with fairness.

Sport as Fairness

The idea and practice of sport I want to suggest is concerned with justice as fairness. Rawls, (1958, p.165) in speaking of justice as fairness, although he is predominantly concerned with the social practice of institutions, recognizes that there is a distinction but none the less a connection between the application of the term fairness to a practice and the application of that term to a particular action by an individual. In his book *A Theory of Justice* he explicates his theory of 'fairness' by reference to two principles: those of freedom and equality (1972). He argues that freedom (or liberty) is a basic human value that rational people in their practices would always want to include and protect and that this right to freedom will always take priority over the principle of equal opportunity. I want to develop this general position of Rawls' in relation to sport and attempt to demonstrate that the practice of sport is not only a just one but essentially (despite its breakdown from time to time) a moral one.

In 'broad' terms, justice as fairness relates to sport with regard to the principle of freedom, by an individual having the right to choose (or reject) which sport(s) he takes up;[5] and in 'narrow' terms by him agreeing to the rules that characterize that sport as being the particular one that it is. In so far as the individual sees his life and moral character bound up and co-existent with the choices he makes, the activities he enters into, the efforts he undergoes, he will see that sport is no less 'serious' than other forms of human practice. The point here is that although a sport may be regarded as a particular kind of practice which is characterized by its rules, it is by no means separate from, or discontinuous with, life or moral concern. It is in fact an identifiable form of life and like the law or medicine, not a morally irrelevant one.[6] Similarly, equality relates to sport in that players of a particular sport come together in the full knowledge that its rules apply to themselves as well as to others. They realize and agree that the rules that apply are in the interest of *all* players and that it is a part of the expected practice of the sport that they will be *impartially* applied so that one player or team will not gain unfair advantage over another. It is on this basis that sport as a competitive practice proceeds. If it was thought that the rules of sport were not concerned with the bringing about of fairness in this sense sport would cease to be the practice it is. The rational agent as player will not only have made a commitment about equality of treatment in advance of being a participant but as a participant will both uphold and submit to what is fair. It will be seen then that fundamental to the concept of fairness in sport is the acknowledgement and acceptance that the rules, which both constitute and govern play, shall not only be agreed to in advance but willingly observed in practice. The point here is that both logically and morally there is only one way to play the game fairly and that is by the rules.[7] Acting unfairly arises not so much from the accidental transgression of the rules so much as in the deliberate breaking of them. The cheat and spoilsport are so called not because they break the rules but because they break them intentionally in the hope of gaining unfair advantage. Such acts are not merely 'illegal', in terms of not conforming to the rules but immoral in that the agreement entered into with others has been broken. Keenan (1975) expresses the point this way:

> If cheating in any form occurs among those parties to the game, they simply fail to adopt the principle of fair play and the morality of justice. (p.117)

The act of breaking the rules in sport is somewhat akin to the making of a promise and then not keeping it: to try to gain unfair advantage by breaking the rules is not to be in sport at all, for the concept of sport implies a constraint on acts done to gain unfair advantage. More than this it recognizes the unfairness of some acts in that although they may be permitted by the rules they actually contravene the spirit of the practice.[8] Acting fairly involves more than merely following the rules: it involves also a commitment to what they stand for in the name of what is fair. The principle of equality in sport expects the acceptance of the duty of fair play by all participants. Those who have grasped the principle will not only have adopted a common set of rules and their spirit but they will understand that it is only by practising them that the aspirations and interests of others as well as themselves can be realized. They will have seen that to recognize another player as a person one must consider him and act towards him in certain ways. This not only leads to the preservation of sport as a practice but has clear implications for how relationships are to be conducted in terms of that practice.

In summarizing the view that sport, like some other socially constituted practices is concerned with justice as fairness, it can be said that it is inherently concerned with the twin principles of freedom and equality. Take these fundamental principles away from sport and the practice as it has been constituted would cease to exist. Sport is just, in so far as all who participate in it, abide by the rules and willingly submit to their binding nature and spirit even when it is possible to gain advantage by not doing so. In important respects fair play in sport lies not so much in the hands of the referee but in the actions of players and the reasons they have for conducting themselves in the way that they do. It will thus be seen that the concept of sport as fairness and the having and forming of character are mutually reinforcing.

Sport and the Development of Moral Character

The character building claims of sport are not unfamiliar. Such admired qualities as loyalty, co-operation, courage, resolution, will-power, self-control, endurance, perseverance and determination are often mentioned as arising from a participation in games and sport. It will be seen, however, that such qualities are not confined or peculiar to them. Taken on their own, however, they may be considered as desirable human traits but which are not in themselves moral. Thieves and murderers for example, may display these same qualities and be admired for them but nobody would wish to say that the practices they engaged upon are moral ones. There is a big difference between the meaning of character in general and the development of an ethical or moral character. The conceptual question that therefore arises is this: Is sport the type of human practice that is logically tied to and consistent with the development of a moral character? If the idea of sport as fairness can be accepted, as outlined, it follows that if one is concerned with its teaching one is *ipso facto* concerned with the morality of its practice and the preservation of its ideals and standards. Sport without a proper understanding of its rules and of the underlying principles upon which those rules are based, would not be and could not be all that it is and should be in terms of moral understanding and conduct. This is a point well recognized by both Aspin (1975) and Meakin (1982). Moral character is developed in sport, as in other spheres of life, insofar as such admired human qualities as loyalty, courage and resolution are cultivated and directed to uphold what is fair and just and in the interest of all. To this extent it can be argued that the practice of sport is commensurate with moral education and the development of a moral character. Without a logical connection with morality sport might well provide a forum for the encouragement and display of admired human virtues but it would not necessarily be in keeping with the development of moral character. To maintain that sport is a moral activity by virtue of the underlying principles, rules and ideals that characterize it, however, is not to maintain that players always and invariably act in a moral way. This they clearly do not always do. The fact that this is so, however, in no way invalidates the conceptual point being made here or of its importance and implication for the educationist.[9]

A further question which sometimes arises is: 'Does the practice of sport demand or provide exceptional opportunities for the nurture and cultivation of such admired human qualities?' In the absence of clear cut empirical evidence about the relative merits of different activities in terms of moral development it is difficult to make a definitive or all embracing judgment and yet if one looks at other forms of socially acceptable activities it is hard to escape the conclusion reached by Maraj (1965, p.107) that:

> There are not many situations in everyday life which provide either the kind of opportunities or the number of them evoking the qualities which are considered desirable, as are provided by sport.

What, it should be noted, is *not* being said here is that such qualities as persistence, initiative and self-reliance are specifically and can only be trained in and through sport or that they can then automatically be transferred and applied to other spheres of life. This latter view is surely a naive and unfounded one of the relationship between sport and the development of character. Indeed it is on this point that Nisbet (1972, p.65) observes that:

> We should not too readily jump to the conclusion that the boy who was courageous or loyal on the rugger field will automatically be courageous or loyal on the shop floor or as father of a family or (as a member) of the House of Commons.

What does seem more reasonable is the suggestion that sport, when seen and taught as a socially constituted practice concerned with fairness, provides an ethically based context of endeavour in which such qualities of character are not only encouraged but are seen to be in keeping with the best traditions of its various instances. Whilst some sports like ski-jumping place a premium on daring, coolness and self-control; others like soccer place an emphasis on cooperative effort, staying power and determination. Whereas (as far as I know) it is empirically unfounded to contend that sport or the sports field is the *best* training ground for the development of admired qualities of character, it does not seem at all unreasonable to suggest that sport provides an unusually good forum for the encouraged display of such qualities which are not only admired in sport but in other aspects of life. Certainly acts of generosity and magnanimity on the sportsfield are universally recognized to be sportsmanlike. Similarly altruistic acts of sportsmanship are not only recognized as befitting a sportsman but also to be morally praiseworthy.[10]

It is not the job of the physical educationist to utilize sport as a *means* of moral education and/or the cultivation of admired qualities of character. Rather he is concerned with initiating children into various kinds of physical activities, some of which are called sport. In teaching sport as a particular kind of human practice, however, it is the physical educationist's responsibility to see that the ethical principles upon which it is based are properly understood and that the manner in which a sport is conducted is in accord with its rules and in keeping with the best traditions of its practice. The physical educationist can guarantee nothing, but as an influential guardian of an ethically based practice he can do a good deal to uphold its highest ideals, its most cherished traditions. As in all forms of learning much depends on the attitudes and judgments that are brought to bear upon what is done and whether what is taught and encouraged, is regarded as worthwhile in the context of life. Like morality, the practice of sport is a species of evaluation, a kind of appraisal of human conduct.

If in the past there was an all too ready assumption that attitudes and qualities encouraged and developed on the sports field were transferable into other areas of life the present position may be regarded as confused and sceptical. It is confused because, as was said earlier, sport is still thought of by some educationists in terms of play and as cut off from life rather than being coextensive with it (Dearden, 1968 and 1969; and Peters, 1966). It is sceptical because there is little or no empirically-based evidence to suggest a positive link between the development of admired qualities and a participation in sports. Observation of some forms and levels of competitive sport, indeed, would even suggest a negative relationship. Helpful and substantiating though it would be to have proof of the effects of the 'transfer of training' arising from a participation in sport to the rest of life, conceptually speaking, nothing greatly hangs upon the provision of such evidence. The fact is, the teaching of sport does and should entail the initiation of children into a form of life which, because it involves the acquisition of skills, the development of practical knowledge, the active nurturing of admired human qualities, as well as moral understanding and conduct, is in effect a form of education.

The development of a moral character in sport is best thought of in terms of a person whose actions are informed and guided by what he knows and understands of the rules and ethical principles upon which those rules are based, as well as by the best traditions of the practice so that fairness and self-formation result.

As has been indicated the Kantian notion of 'self-formation' (1960, pp.2–3) that can take place in sport is an important one. It goes beyond the idea of a passive compliance with the rules and an acceptance of decision-making and judgment by the referee. It suggests rather a rational and autonomous commitment to uphold the values of the practice and a demonstrated willingness and authenticity to abide by the rules in the interests of fair play. It is by understanding that the practice of sport is essentially a moral one that the player accepts and learns to regulate his play in the interests of all. Not to accept personal responsibility for how the practice is to be conducted and leave it entirely to the referee is an abrogation of self-command, a denial of the opportunity for self-formation.[11] If the development of a moral character in sport means anything it is concerned with the individual player being self-governed in the sense not only of determining what he is going to do, but of determining what he *should* do in terms of what is fair. If the idea of sport as an ethically based form of human practice is to be preserved it places considerable emphasis upon getting players to accept responsibility for what they do.

What then can be concluded from what has been said about sport, moral education and the development of character? It is this: that sport in common with education is inherently concerned with the moral no less than with the rational. Sport, at least in so far as it entails the promotion of practical knowledge and moral conduct, is educative. The formation and having of character in sport, as in the rest of life, is concerned with the person in all his concrete makeup — his beliefs, attitudes and behaviour. To develop a moral character does not mean the identification and cultivation of a few desirable traits which are encouraged and demanded in a number of given situations: it means rather to assist individuals towards self-formation in a principled, authentic and discerning manner, whether on or off the gamesfield.

Notes

1 For the present purpose I shall use sport hereafter to refer predominantly to 'game' sports which are rule-governed and team activities.
2 See also: Lucas (1959, p.11) and Callois (1961).
3 Somewhat perplexingly Dearden (1965, p.97) also lists 'a love of nature and pitting oneself against the hazards' as being serious in that they are culturally valued. Thus outdoor pursuits and some forms of sport like sailing and climbing might also be considered 'serious'.
4 It is worth noting that although Huizinga (1970, p.28) speaks of play as 'self contained' he also sees that the relationship of play and seriousness is 'always fluid' and not at all simple. His main thesis, it should not be forgotten, is concerned with showing that play is an essential element in all highly regarded activities, and may in some senses be the basis of them all.
5 The matter of whether or not school games should be compulsory is an important one since it raises the question of whether or not something which is compulsory can be justified in terms of the principle of freedom.

I do not propose to enter this controversy here apart from saying, along with some educationists, that it is first necessary to initiate children into an activity albeit compulsorily, before providing them with the choice of whether it is in their best interests to continue with it.

For further comment on this point and related ones see chapter 5.

6   Two articles which are of interest here and touch upon the 'serious' and 'non-serious' aspects of play and games and have implications for sport are by Kolnai (1965–66, pp.103–8) and Midgley (1974, pp.231–53).

7   This thesis has recently been challenged, see Lehman (1981).

8   For a clear exposition of why this is so see Fraleigh (1982 and 1984).

9   For a helpful reminder that teachers in schools are a profession and that this entails the making of ethical judgments in relation to what one is teaching see Shea (1978).

10   Sportsmanship is a more complex phenomenon than at first appears. For a discussion of its different meanings as well as its moral implications see Arnold (1984b). See also chapter 4.

11   For greater elaboration on this point see Arnold (1984a, p.280).

4 The Social and Moral Implications of Sportsmanship

A part of the tradition of sport, especially as it was practised in the English public schools of the nineteenth century, was the idea of sportsmanship. It is a term to which reference is often made but to which little explanation is given. The last serious attempt to examine its meaning was something like twenty years ago.[1] Recent writers on sport, it would appear, have studiously ignored its relevance to the way in which competitive sport *should* be conducted. Even McIntosh (1979, p.1), who in his book *Fair Play*, sets out 'to link an analysis of the ethics of sport with the theory and practice of education', makes only passing comment on it. What follows, therefore, is an attempt to help rectify what I see as a neglected dimension in contemporary discussion of the relationship between sport and education, especially in the general area of social and moral development.

Sportsmanship, although most readily associated with particular types of commendatory acts done in the context of sport, is sometimes extended to apply to other spheres of life and living, especially those which are concerned with competing fairly and honestly as well as with good humour. I do not propose to embark upon these latter applications but to concentrate upon what I see to be its central cases all of which are to do with the actions and conduct of sportsmen and sportswomen when engaged in sport. There are, it seems to me, essentially three different if related views about sportsmanship and I propose looking at each of these in turn. They are:

    (i)   sportsmanship as a form of social union;
    (ii) sportsmanship as a means in the promotion of pleasure; and
    (iii) sportsmanship as a form of altruism.

Each view has implications for the role of the educator.

It should be made clear that although I shall be looking at each of these views separately and in turn for purposes of exposition I do not necessarily wish to maintain that they are not to some extent overlapping or that in any one person at different times (and maybe even at the same time) all three views cannot be partially represented.

First, it would be helpful to make a preliminary comment. The idea of sport as fairness, it will be recalled, maintains that when a player enters into the institutionalized social practice of a sport he tacitly agrees to abide by the rules which characterize and govern it.[2] It recognizes further that if the practice of sport is to be preserved and flourish a great deal is dependent upon the players and officials understanding and acting in accord with what is fair. They will accept and realize that breaches of the rules, especially if flagrant and deliberate, will destroy the very activity that they have agreed to participate in and uphold. They will appreciate also that if 'fairness' is interpreted too contractually or legalistically there is always the danger that that aspect of sport known as 'sportsmanship' will be construed as being concerned only with these acts which demonstrate a ready acceptance of the rules and a willingness to abide by them. It will be seen, however, that this is a reasonable expectation of all players and the notion of sportsmanship connotes something more. What must be emphasized is that fairness, if understood only in its formal rule — following sense, can only be regarded as a necessary condition of sportsmanship but by no means a sufficient one. This point applies to all three views of sportsmanship I intend to outline.

Sportsmanship as a Form of Social Union

The idea of sport as a social union takes into account, but goes beyond, an agreement to willingly abide and play by the rules in the interests of what is fair. It is also concerned with the preservation and furtherance of its best traditions, customs and conventions so that the community which makes up the social union can not only cooperatively participate in sport but successfully relate to one another as persons through an understood, shared and appreciated mode of proceeding. It is of interest to note that *The Sportsmanship Brotherhood* (*Literary Digest*, 1926, pp.60–1), which was founded in 1926, whilst itself was indebted to the English public school ethos of games playing, may be regarded as a forerunner to this view. Its aim was to foster and spread the spirit of sportsmanship throughout the world which it saw, in part at least, as a form of social and moral well-being. By adopting the slogan 'Not that you won or lost — but that you played the game', it brought home that point that the *manner* in which sport is conducted is no less important than its outcome, if amicability and brotherhood are to be encouraged and upheld. Rawls (1973, pp.525–6), in speaking of games as a simple instance of a social union, suggests that in addition to it being concerned with its rules, it is also concerned with an agreed and cooperative 'scheme of conduct in which the excellences and enjoyments of each (player) are complementary to the good of all'. The idea of sport as a social union then is not just concerned with getting players to accept and abide by the rules but also with the maintenance and extolling of a way of life in which sportsmen find value, cooperation and mutual satisfaction. If this view of sportsmanship is to flourish and be furthered it is not a matter of merely adopting a particular code of etiquette or set of shibboleths, but of having a genuine commitment to the values of fellowship and goodwill which are held to be more important than the desire to win or the achievement of victory. The central purpose of the social union view of sportsmanship is to preserve and uphold fraternal relationships that can arise in, and through, a participation in sport. More than this, it sees this purpose as being intrinsically involved with the nature of sport itself. Any attempt, therefore, to characterize the nature of sport without reference to it would leave the concept and practice of sport incomplete and considerably impoverished. It is this point which, if properly understood by teachers, can help prevent sport degenerating, as it does from time to time, into a form of anti-social or even violent conflict. It is important to stress that the social union view of sportsmanship is not to be seen merely as a socially cohesive device in order to help regulate and oil the institutional practice of sport, though this effect may well come about. Rather it should be perceived as a community of individuals united by a particular practice in which the arts of chivalry are practised in the interests of mutual affection, comraderie and fellowship. It will be seen by the participants, with the encouragement of teachers, as the kind of practice which places a high premium upon those qualities and forms of conduct such as good humour, respect, politeness and affability which are conducive to, rather than destructive of good interpersonal relations and cooperative, if competitive endeavour. In other words the idea of sport as a social union is a particular kind of social system in and by which players and officials come together in order to share a commonly valued form of life, one part of which is concerned with the manner in which one should ideally participate if the system is to flourish.[3] An example of this is provided by an incident at the French tennis championships of 1982; when Wilander, the Swedish player, was awarded match point against his opponent Clerc on the grounds that a drive down the line was out, Wilander instead of accepting the umpire's decision, as the rules state, asked for the point to be played again because he thought the ball was 'good and that he didn't have a chance'. Mr Dorfman, the referee, at some risk to his official position but conscious of the good of the players and game alike, agreed (Bellamy, 1982, p.10).[4] Another example comes from the World Athletic championships of 1983, when Banks, the American world triple jump record holder, was defeated in the last round by the Pole Hoffman. Instead of being grieved and withdrawn as is often the case, when victory eludes an athlete by a hair's breadth, Banks demonstrated his delight at Hoffman's success by running round the track with him as an act of respect and comraderie. For both a moment between them had been forged. What is clear is that the system requires of all members a commitment to live out the ideals cherished by the union in a way that predisposes towards its convivial continuance. When sport is viewed in this way sportsmanship can be seen as an evaluative term which is attributed to those who not only uphold and play according to the rules but keep faith with their spirit by acts and forms of conduct which are not required by the rules but which are freely made in accordance with the best traditions of competitive but friendly rivalry. This is a part of the heritage of sport into which all school children should be initiated. The social union view of sport then, apart from a ready acceptance of what is fair, sees acts of sportsmanship as chiefly having to do with maintaining the best traditions of sport as a valued and shared form of life. On this view sportsmanship is more in keeping with a particular kind of socialization or ideology which predisposes group members to act in ways that are supported and admired by the social union of which they are an integral part. Because of this the social union view of sportsmanship is best understood as being more to do with an idealized form or model of group mores rather than as an individual and principled form of morality.

Sportsmanship as a Means in the Promotion of Pleasure

Keating's (1979) analysis of sportsmanship, although it has some things in common with the idea of sport as a social union, arises more from the etymological meaning of sport which in essence, he maintains is:

a kind of diversion which has for its direct and immediate end fun, pleasure and delight and which is dominated by a spirit of moderation and generosity. (p.265)

He contrasts sport with athletics which he says:

is essentially a competitive activity, which has for its end victory in the contest and which is marked by a spirit of dedication, sacrifice and intensity. (*ibid*)

What it is important to realize is that when Keating speaks of 'sport' and 'athletics' he does not necessarily have in mind a difference between particular activities (for example, field games and track and field) so much as an attitude or motivation towards them (1973, p.167). With the term 'sport', he associates the notion of play and the doing of something for its own sake, and with the notion of 'athletics' he associates the notion of contest and the struggle for victory.

I do not intend to dwell upon the difficulties of holding such a simplistic either/or position. Nonetheless, in the interests of clarity, a few brief comments seem desirable. First, whilst it may be true that play is more readily associated with some activities than with others, it should not be assumed that play is confined to them or that play can be adequately expressed only in terms of them. Play can enter 'serious' activities, like war, just as it can enter 'non-serious' ones like games. Second, the fact that an activity is 'competitive' does not necessarily preclude having a play attitude towards it. This point holds true even when recognizing that a preoccupation with winning can sometimes inhibit, even neutralize, a play spirit. To acknowledge this however, is not to say, as Keating suggests, that if an activity is competitive it necessarily follows that a given attitude accompanies it.[5] Third, it is needlessly confusing to imply, as Keating does, that 'athletics' is concerned with competition whereas 'sport' is not. The fact is most, if not all, physical activities commonly known as sports are competitive in one sense or another. This is a logical, if trivial point, about them. In view of this it might have been said less perplexingly that the 'sportsman's' attitude towards that family of physical activities known as sport differs from that of the 'athlete's'. This difference in attitude, however, stems not from the constitutive nature of the activities themselves, as Keating suggests,[6] (1979, p.266 and 1973, p.170) but rather from the way they are viewed by those who participate in them. Fourth, it does not follow either, as is suggested by some other writers,[7] that his motives are necessarily undesirable or immoral in some way. There is a big distinction, for example, between a contestant setting out to gain an honourable victory and a contestant setting out to defeat at all costs (and maybe to humiliate) an opponent.[8]

Having made these observations it would be helpful now to examine and comment upon, accepting for the moment Keating's two ways of regarding competitive activities, what amounts to two ways of looking at sportsmanship. It would seem that for the 'athlete' given his goal of 'exclusive possession' rather than cooperative endeavour, sportsmanship can never be much more than a means of taking some of the rawness out of competitive strife. Its purpose is to mitigate the effects of what is seen as a confrontation and challenge between two adversaries. Sportsmanship in these circumstances, Keating seems to be saying, can only ease, soften and in some way make more civilized, what is essentially a contest between two prize fighters. This is perhaps particularly so in sports like boxing and wrestling. The athlete will see the need for disciplined conduct and self-control, even courtesy, but he will not be inclined towards expressions of cordiality or generosity. Sportsmanship for the athlete above all means achieving victory in a dignified and honourable way. He will see the need for 'an impartial and equal following of the rules' and the need for 'modesty in victory and quiet composure in defeat, but that is all. 'Fairness or fair play', says Keating, (1973) is 'the pivotal virtue in athletics' (p.170). His chief and driving motive, however, will be the outcome of 'winning' rather than amicability or joy. In summary Keatings' presentation of sportsmanship in athletics seems pretty well commensurate with the idea of sport as justice and which, as I suggested, should be an expectation of all participants. It should not perhaps therefore be regarded as a genus of sportsmanship at all. It meets minimal requirements but no more than this.

For the '*sportsman*', on the other hand, sportsmanship becomes something more expansive. Here sportsmanship is more than simply following a legislative code (which the justice theory of sport might be accused, wrongly of being); nor is it best understood as being represented by those virtues which often accompany the admired player such as courage, endurance, perseverance, self-control, self-reliance, sang-froid, and self-respect (with which the character development theory of sport is largely associated). Rather it is concerned with those 'moral habits or qualities' which are essentially and characteristically to do with generosity and magnanimity (Keating, 1979, p.266). Unlike the merely 'just' player the true sportsman adopts a cavalier attitude towards his rights as permitted by the code. Instead he prefers to be magnanimous and self-sacrificing if, by such conduct, 'he contributes to the fun of the occasion' (*ibid*). It is important to see in Keating's account of sport that competition is not so much seen in logical terms of 'exclusive possession', by one or the other of the vying parties, but more in terms of a cooperative enterprise, which is seen to be a potentially shared source of pleasure. For Keating then, sportsmanship for the sportsman, is essentially a desirable or efficacious manner or way of acting in sport which is in keeping with the promotion of pleasure and the spirit of play.

From the moral point of view at least three questions arise from Keating's account of sportsmanship. The first is: Can sportsmanship in relation to sport be considered moral if it is seen only as a *means* or as an instrument in the promotion of pleasure? The answer to this question is very much closely related to whether or not he is taking a utilitarian stance towards moral issues and this he does not make clear.

The second question is concerned with the sense in which Keating uses the phrase sportsmanship as a 'moral category'. If he means it in the sense of being 'self-contained'[9], then it cannot properly be said to be moral since it is inapplicable to life outside of sport. Similarly if he wants to regard it as a form of play, as he seems to, then at least at one level of analysis, it is 'non-serious' as opposed to 'serious' and therefore non-moral in consequence. If, one the other hand, he is intending that sportsmanship is concerned with the type of actions that fall within the general category of the moral and therefore somehow related to the 'business of life' this should have been stated more explicitly. If this is the case, however, the problem remains as to how this interpretation is to be reconciled with the notion of play. One way round this dilemma might be to say that although play is generally regarded as a non-serious affair this is not to say that players cannot take what they are doing seriously (in the psychological sense) or that serious incidents (for example, death, injury or acts of malevolence) cannot occur. To say, in other words, that play as a category is non-serious and therefore non-moral, is to say that this is the way it is best understood but recognizing, at the same time, that things occasionally occur that transform it momentarily into something else, which may or may not have moral significance.

The third question is related to the first one. Even if utilitarianism is adopted as a general ethical theory, it is not clear why conduct that is conducive to fun is necessarily more pleasurable and therefore more moral than conduct that is conducive to 'honourable victory'. One is tempted to ask here, is it not the case that the best examples of sportsmanship in terms of generosity and magnanimity arise out of the pursuit of 'honourable victory'? A case which gives some support to this thesis is when Brasher, at the Melbourne Olympic Games in

1956, was disqualified from winning the 3000 metres steeplechase for allegedly hindering his opponents. The point here is that it was these same athletes (Rosznyoi, Laresen and Loufer) who protested on Brasher's behalf and got the decision reversed, thus sacrificing the medals they would otherwise have won.

All in all Keating's attempt to look at sportsmanship in terms of 'athletics' and 'sport' by reference competition, or its relative absence, is not altogether clear or helpful. It is not helpful from the educational point of view especially, because it firstly reduces sport to be but a means in the pursuit of pleasure; and secondly, in doing so, it forgoes any intrinsically worthwhile claims along the lines earlier suggested it undoubtedly has. What Keating's analysis does underline, however, is the importance of the play spirit that can and should be encouraged to occur in sport and the desirable attributes of magnanimity and generosity which are associated with it.

Sportsmanship as a Form of Altruism

It should be apparent by now that the term sportsmanship and its relation to sport and morality is a more complex and subtle one than is commonly supposed. In the social union view of sportsmanship it was suggested that sportsmanship has largely to do with the preservation and exemplification of a valued form of life which puts a premium upon an idealized and amicable way of participating. The pleasure view of sportsmanship as being chiefly and characteristically concerned with generous and magnanimous conduct that is conducive to the promotion of fun and pleasure. The view of sportsmanship I shall now present takes a different stance. This view is concerned more with seeing sportsmanship as a form of altruistically motivated conduct that is concerned with the good or welfare of another. Again it should be stressed that I do not see these three views of sportsmanship as mutually exclusive. I see them rather as providing a different focus or perspective on a form of social phenomenon which is essentially both recognizable and understood.

What then, more precisely, is the altruistic view of sportsmanship and how and in what way, if at all, can it be considered as a moral form of conduct? In order to look at the second part of the question first I propose to contrast the Kantian view of morality with what I shall call the altruistic view. For Kant, morality is primarily a matter of reason and rationality. It resides in and is based upon the adoption of principles which are universalizable, impartial, consistent and obligatory. It emphasizes choice, decision, will and thoughtful deliberation.[10] Williams (1976), in writing of the Kantian tradition, points out that:

> the moral point view is specially characterized by its impartiality and its indifference to any particular relations to particular persons and that moral thought requires abstraction from particular circumstances and particular characteristics of the parties, including the agent, except in so far as these can be universal features of any morally similar situation. (p.198)

Williams continues:

> the motivations of a moral agent, correspondingly, involve a rational application of impartial principle and are thus different in kind from sorts of motivations that he might have for treating some particular persons differently because he happened to have some particular interest towards them. (*ibid*)

It will be seen that the Kantian view of morality has a lot in common with the justice theory of sport as well as with those preconditional features of sportsmanship which are to do with fairness. In stressing the universal and impartial, however, the Kantian view seems to overlook or disregard some aspects of interpersonal relations which are as morally important in sport as in other spheres of life. I refer to such virtues as sympathy, compassion, concern and friendship. What needs to be clarified is that the 'moral point of view', whilst importantly connected with the impartial and obligatory, is by no means totally taken up by them. This is perhaps particularly so in the education of the young. In speaking of sportsmanship then as a form of altruism I am particularly concerned to show that sportsmanship in this sense, whilst obligated to the following of impartial rules which govern play, at the same time gives moral scope to go beyond them. In order to say more about this and at the same time point up the differences between the Kantian view of morality and those aspects of morality and sportsmanship that place greater emphasis upon the importance of personal and particular relationships, I propose to look now at sportsmanship as a form of altruism. At the same time I shall indicate that acts of supererogation are more in keeping with the Kantian view than with the altruistic view.

Altruism is perhaps best understood as having to do with those forms of action and conduct that are not done merely because of what is fair and just in terms of playing and keeping to the rules but because, in addition, there is a genuine concern for, an interest in, and concern for one's fellow competitors, whether on the same side or in opposition. At first sight it may seem as if sportsmanship in this altruistic sense has to do with supererogatory acts in that they go beyond duty or what the rules expect. In common with other forms of supererogatory acts, supererogatory acts in sport are to do as Hare (1981) puts it with those acts which are 'praiseworthy but not obligatory' (p.198). Put another way, to say that an act in sport is supererogatory is to say two things about it. First, the sportsman is not morally (or by rule) obliged to perform it. He is, in other words, permitted not to perform it. Second, the action is morally praiseworthy; it would be commendable if it were performed. Urmson (1958), in speaking of the need to make room for moral actions which lie outside the realm of the obligation, could well be speaking of the kinds of situation with which the sportsman is confronted. He argues that there is a large range of actions whose moral status is insufficiently expressible in terms of the traditional classification of actions into morally impermissible, morally neutral, and morally obligatory and that it is necessary to allow 'for a range of actions which are of moral value and which an agent may feel called upon to perform, but which cannot be demanded and whose omission cannot be called wrongdoing' (p.208).

There seem to be at least two ways in sport in which an act can go beyond duty (or the demands of fair play). The first way is by acting out of concern for the other or at some risk, cost or sacrifice to oneself. An example here might be the marathon runner who, at the cost of victory, stops to help a fellow runner in a state of distress. The second way is by acting on behalf of another so that more good is brought about than if one had merely acted out of duty or in accordance with the rules. An actual case is provided by Meta Antenan, who although leading in a long jump competition against her great German rival, asked of the presiding jury that her opponent have a longer rest period than is provided by the rules, because of her having just taken part in another event[11] (Borotra, 1978, p.8).

Such examples of sportsmanship, it might be thought, are both supererogatory and altruistic in that they go beyond what is required by duty or a proper observance of the rules but it should be pointed out that although acts of supererogation and altruism have certain things in common — namely that they have moral value and that they are not morally obligatory — they also have certain important differences which prevent one being assimilated to the other. Whereas supererogatory acts tend to stem from a traditional framework dominated by the notions of duty and obligation, and by some writers

(Grice, 1967, chapter 4) are even spoken of as 'ultra obligations', altruistic acts are best perceived as belonging to an entirely different realm of moral experience. Whereas supererogatory acts are seen as 'doing more than duty requires' in a sacrificial or enobling sort of way, altruistic acts are prompted by various forms of altruistic emotion. Whereas the 'supererogatory' sportsman may be prompted into acts which, to him, have the force of duty, but which he would not recognize as being encumbent on others, the 'altruistic' sportsman may be prompted into acts by the emotions of concern and care.[12]

In referring to the two examples of 'going beyond duty' forms of sportsmanship cited above, it will be seen that either or both could either be considered 'supererogatory' or 'altruistic'. The correct interpretation would depend upon the considerations or states which prompted them. Moral actions in sport, like other actions, cannot be properly understood only by reference to their external form.

It will be seen then that supererogatory or altruistic forms of sportsmanship are essentially different from those forms which are to do with a conventionalized set of values to do with preservation of amicability and group harmony or with the successful pursuit of pleasure.

What characterizes altruistic forms of sportsmanship particularly is that sympathy, compassion and concern are directed towards the other in virtue of his or her suffering, travail, misery or pain. The altruistic sportsman not only thinks about and is affected by the plight of the other but acts in such a way that is directed to bring help or comfort in some way. Altruistic acts of sportsmanship stem from a desire for the other's good. This sometimes leads to impulsive or spontaneous forms of conduct that arise from the sporting context as when, for example, Karpati the Hungarian fencer reached out and tried to console a defeated and disappointed opponent. Such acts, it will be seen, are not motivated by such Kantian virtues as obligation and duty so much as by a perceptive and human response to another's plight. On the rationalistic Kantian view such acts based on altruistic emotions would be considered unreliable as moral motives because they are too transitory, changeable, maybe emotionally charged and not sufficiently detached, impartial and consistent. Yet the question arises are they less moral on account of this? Blum, (1980, p.93) who has addressed himself to this very problem argues, for instance, 'that the domain in which morally good action takes the form of universalizable principles of obligation does not exhaust the areas of morally good action'. He argues further that there are different kinds of virtues. Some are articulated by the Kantian view — justice, impartiality, conscientiousness and so on while others such as kindness, concern and compassion are articulated better by the altruistic view (*ibid*).

Whereas the Kantian view is predominantly concerned with what is right and what is just for all, the altruistic view is more concerned with the good of the other even if this sometimes means acting particularly and personally rather than objectively and impartially and/or in a strict accordance with what the rules decree. All in all the altruistic view of sportsmanship in contrast to the social union view or the pursuit of pleasure view arises not from a concern for the pre- servation of a valued and particular form of interpersonal of life or the promotion of pleasure as an ethic but rather from a particular and genuine concern for another's welfare. When acts in sport go beyond that which is expected of players generally and are done only out of concern for another's good and for no other reason, they are not only altruistic but exemplify the best traditions of sportsmanship. They also help characterize what it is to be morally educated.

Notes

1　Keating's article (1979, pp.264–71) first appeared in *Ethics*, 75, (1964), pp.25–35.
2　For an interesting article along these lines see Keenan (1975, pp.115–9).
3　This conception of the way sport can (or should) be conducted is not out of keeping with what some writers have referred to as the 'radical ethic' which recognizes that 'the excellence of the outcome as important, but holds equally important the way that excellence is achieved' (see Scott, 1973, pp.75–7). It also holds that 'the winning of the game is subser- vient to the playing of the game' in which such qualities as 'corporate loyalty and respect for others' are encouraged. All in all 'The game is viewed as a framework within which various aims may be realized, qualities fostered, needs met, and values upheld' see Kew (1978, pp.104– 7).
4　Two points can be made about this incident. The first is that Wilander, on being asked about why he had challenged the umpire's decision, replied that he could not accept a win 'like that' by which he was taken to mean not only unfairly but in a way which would have brought dishon- our to himself, and discredit from his opponent, who also thought his drive was in, as well as from his fellow circuit players.
5　See Gallie (1955–56, pp.167–98) who argued that competition is a normative concept and as such is open to being contested since the evaluative frameworks surrounding it (for example, a 'Lombardian ethic', where winning is everything, as opposed to the 'radical ethic', referred to in note 3 above) are sometimes irreconcilable.

6 Fraleigh (1975, pp.74–82) has touched upon some of the complexities of this issue.

7 Bailey (1975, pp.40–50) argues that since competitive games are concerned with winning, especially when they are made compulsory, they are not only morally questionable but morally undesirable in that those behaviours and attitudes that are conducive to the defeat of the other side and all that this implies for both the winner and loser.

8 Arnold (1982, pp.126–30) attempts to refute Bailey's view of competition and point out the difference between 'trying to win' when competing and the attitude and outcome of 'winning at all costs'. He also points out the intrinsic values of competitive games.

9 For an explication of play seen in this way see Huizinga (1970, p.32), Lucas (1959, p.11) and Schmitz (1979, pp.22–8) among others.

10 Consult Beck (1959) for a good statement of the Kantian position.

11 As a result she lost the competition by one centimetre.

12 Lyons (1983, pp.125–45), in keeping with the points I am making, speaks about a 'morality of response and care'. This she contrasts with a 'morality of justice', which stems more from the Kantian tradition, grounded in obligations and duty.

5 Competitive Sport, Winning and Education

The nature and significance of competition in education, despite ongoing discussion on the matter, remains a controversial one. The issues are wide ranging and cannot be fully entered into here. They do, however, have a bearing upon the place of competitive sport, especially in the context of moral education, and because of this it is proposed that something should be said first about competition in relation to education in general before looking at it in relation to sport in particular.

Competition as a Contested Concept

It is sometimes said that competition is an 'essentially contested' normative concept. That is to say what is understood by the term derives from incompatible value systems so that no single coherent analysis is possible[1]. Each value system makes its interpretation in accordance with what it claims to be 'convincing arguments, evidence and other forms of justification' (Gallie, 1964, p.157). In this respect competition is like other contested concepts such as 'art' and 'democracy'. Broadly speaking, however, it can be said that there are two views about competition: the positivist view and the negativist view. The positivist view is one that holds that competition is a pre-condition of personal development and social progress and that it provides a framework from which benefits and burdens can be distributed fairly and freely. Such a framework, it is argued, is necessary if such qualities as initiative, resource and independence are to be fostered and preserved. The negativist view on the other hand, maintains that competitive situations threaten cooperative ventures and help undermine worthwhile personal and social relationships and form a vicious distinction between winners and losers. Competition, it is said, is often the source of envy, despair, selfishness, pride and callousness.

When these ideologically opposed views about competition are discussed in the context of education it is perhaps not surprising that there are those who are for it and those who are against it. Prvulovich (1982), for example, a supporter of competition, writes:

> competition can and does bring out new talents, often un-dreamt of, and in its various forms caters for different abilities, talents and skills. Moreover it encourages new ventures, and whets the appetite for more knowledge and deeper self-fulfilment. (pp.82–3)

Conversely, Fielding (1976), who is a representative of the negativist view, writes:

> I reject the use of competition in schools: competition as a social ideal seems to me abhorrent; competition as a procedural device is morally repugnant because whatever other criteria one wishes to include or omit I would insist that part of one's characterization contains some reference to working against others in a spirit of selfishness. (p.140)

Dearden (1976), perhaps in an effort to provide a neutral analytic account of competition in the face of general value-laden statements such as those above, posits three separately necessary and jointly sufficient conditions for A and B to be in competition for X:

(i)   A and B must both want X. There must be some common object desired by both.
(ii) A's gaining of X must exclude B's gaining possession of it.
(iii) Both A and B should persist in trying to gain exclusive possession of X even when they know that one of them must be excluded. (p.114)

This 'simplifying scheme' of Dearden's, as he calls it, although helpful to a point, omits too many other relevant considerations to be of universal use. It has been criticized by Fielding (1976) on two main grounds. The first is that the 'essentialist methodology' (ie, one that attempts to characterize competition by identifying a set of logically necessary and sufficient conditions) is just too simplistic. Each condition, he maintains, because of the value ladened nature of the term can be 'sensibly challenged' (p.126). The point here is that an essentialist methodology is inappropriate to the task of characterizing competition because it cannot be done whilst remaining impartial to one of the rival views on offer. The second of Fielding's criticisms is on substantive grounds (ie, in terms of what is both raised and more particularly omitted in discussion about the use of the term[2]). He also makes the point that it is also important when dealing with an appraisive concept such as competition that some attention be given to its historical career. He quotes MacIntyre (1971) in support of the view that:

> We cannot investigate a philosophical subject matter adequately unless we take seriously the fact that such a subject matter always has a historical dimension. That dimension is missing in most work by philosophers in the analytic tradition. (p.95)

It is because I consider all three points not only valid in relation to Dearden's analysis of competition but more importantly it is because they are necessary to an understanding of competition in sport in the context of education that they will be borne in mind in the sections that follow.

Competitive Sport and Education

Meakin (1986), in taking account of both Dearden's and Fielding's work on competition, examines what he presents as being the 'strong' and 'weak' critiques that are often levelled against the moral desirability of having competitive sport as a part of compulsory educational curriculum. It is proposed to look at each of these in turn.

The Strong Critique and a Answer to it

The strong critique against competition in schools, especially when it is compulsory is that competition per se is wrong. The claim is that it is intrinsically immoral and leads to selfish and egotistical forms of behaviour. Competitive sport is often seen as a prime example of these tendencies and as a result attracts a good deal of moral censure. As Meakin (*ibid*) expresses it:

> The target of this censure is the undesirable behaviour of many competitors; a bad temperedness that often erupts into violence, a petulant reluctance to accept decisions of umpires and referees, a tendency to bend the rules and commit outright fouls and, more generally, an unsportsmanlike behaviour towards opponents. (p.59)

The strong case against competitive sport in schools then is that it is inherently immoral and that it causes and reinforces undesirable social values and conduct.

Before examining this view of competitive sport it would be helpful if some general comments were made about the presence or otherwise of compulsion in relation to competition in the context of education. Two points are of underlying importance. The first is, as has previously been indicated, that normally speaking moral choices are free choices. The question arises therefore whether curriculum subjects, if they are made compulsory, are in keeping with morality and moral education? On the face of it, it would seem not. If what is considered important in learning and education is not made compulsory, however, how can educational aims and objectives be rationally implemented? It is, of course, possible to take the view that education can and should proceed on the basis that only when a pupil is attracted to a subject or has agreed willingly to enter into it. At least two points can be made against this position, however. The first is that some pupils may never be attracted to a given subject no matter what efforts are made to point out its intrinsic or instrumental values. Should it therefore just be disregarded? The second point is that in any case, the only way of finding out whether a subject has something about it that is rewarding or beneficial in some way, is to try it by engaging in it. An alternative view is that it is only by initiating pupils into what are considered the worthwhile activities of a culture compulsorily, if necessary, at least up to a given age, can they later make a responsible and informed choice about what they most want to do. As White (1982) observes, in order to become free a pupil 'must pass through a period of compulsory education' (p.132). It is only when a sufficient grounding has been given in a range of selected pursuits that a pupil is able to make a free and more informed choice about whether or not he wishes to carry on with them.

In looking at these two views, it seems to me, that the latter one is the more sound, both on moral and pragmatic grounds. In principle and in practice it is likely to prove the more secure way of promoting the interests of a pupils's educational growth and development.

In returning then to the main question of competition it will be recalled that it is often important to provide some historical perspective on how a term has come to be used and understood. This is certainly the case in relation to sport. Originally, *com-petitio* meant 'to question, to strive together'. It was more closely tied to friendship than to rivalry. Competition in the context of sport was, and for many still is, seen as a struggle for excellence,[3] a form of excellence that would not be possible were it not for the type of situation that sport provides. To compete in sport, as has previously been pointed out, it is first necessary to understand the activity and agree to abide by the rules which govern it. If a competitor deliberately breaks or flouts the rules it can be seriously questioned whether what is done remains sport. The point here is that competitive sport is not an unbridled form of conflict, as it is sometimes depicted, but a rule-governed institutionalized practice which attempts to regulate what is permitted and not permitted along lines which are just to all. Additionally, it is reinforced by a set of social conventions and codes of behaviour that are traditionally expected to form a part of a 'sporting' competition. Paradoxically competitive sport is best exemplified as being a rule-governed form of friendly rivalry, which involves cooperation. Perry's (1975) observation that 'Competitions require us to assume the capacity to cooperate if they are to run at all' (p. 128) is perhaps particularly true of sporting ones. To say then that a game is competitive does not necessarily mean that cooperation between the two contestants or two sides is absent; rather it demands that it is present, at least in some degree, if competitive sport as an institutional practice is to continue.

It is perhaps in the longstanding movement known as Olympism that the approach to competitive sport is best enshrined. It stresses the ethic of fair play and sportsmanship and upholds the view that competition should be marked by honest endeavour and goodwill. Far from seeing competitive sport as immoral and anti-social, it sees it as a form of contest that generates fellowship in a mutual struggle for excellence. This picture of competitive sport, it will be seen, is something of an ideal but it is one which has been and remains a part of the story of competitive sport. Whether or not this ideal is lived out as a part of a young person's upbringing is largely, if not entirely, a matter of how competitive sport is promoted and taught in schools. What then is being rejected, both on conceptual and historical grounds, is the view that competitive sport is inherently and therefore necessarily immoral.

The question of selfishness

A serious charge that remains, however, is that competitive sport leads to selfish behaviour. It will be recalled that Fielding (1976) rejected competition in schools on the grounds that led 'to working against others in a spirit of selfishness' (pp. 140–1). Now, although in terms of an outcome of a game it can be said that one person's victory is another person's defeat; or, alternatively, one person's gain is another's loss, does it follow that selfishness is involved?

In view of what has already been said the answer to this must surely be no. In the first place, as has already been noted, competitive sport takes place within a framework of constitutive rules which are applicable to all participants. These rules are aimed at safeguarding the interests of everyone by being fair. Secondly the ideal of 'the good competition', which is perhaps best characterized by acts of sportsmanship, demands not only that each competitor plays fairly in accordance with the rules but that he acts as much in the interests of others as well as himself. Unless all participants agree to cooperate in these respects sport as a valued social institution will cease to exist.

It will be noted that the conceptual points just made about what competitive sport is not only helps refute the view that it is inherently immoral, but when taken together provide normative standards so that appraisals in relation to conduct in sport can take place. Without a clear identification of what competitive sport is little can be done about evaluating it as it is actually practised.

What has been argued is that the traditional view of sport is not, by virtue of the fact that it is competitive, necessarily selfish. This is, of course, not to deny that the motivations of some individual participants may not be selfish. A competitor in sport, as in other walks of life, may be so concerned about his own interests that he disregards or excludes the interests of others. A cricket captain, for example, may be so concerned about scoring a hundred runs for his own glory that he forgoes the chance for his team to win the match by not declaring before he had done so. A rugby centre-three-quarter may be so intent on scoring the winning try himself that he denies his wing the chance of securing victory for the team. Such acts, of course, are selfish and they are not considered in keeping with good sportsmanlike behaviour.

What can be concluded from the above discussion is that at an individual or psychological level there is no denying that acts of selfishness can and do sometimes take place in sport but when they do they are not condoned. What needs to be distinguished is the idea of sport and how it ought to be conducted on the one hand and the fact that this is not always carried out on the other.

The question of winning

A further aspect of the strong critique against competitive sport is the question of winning. In order to look at this more fully, in relation to what has already been said, it will be convenient to outline and then comment upon an article by Bailey (1975) in which he attacks and condemns the point of winning in the playing of games.[4] It is of particular interest in this context because it raises a number of other issues of concern to the educationist that can be profitably discussed.

Bailey begins his article by expressing doubts about the 'appropriateness of competitive games as a part of compulsory general education'. He is particularly sceptical of the view 'that competitive games are generally educative' (*ibid*, p.40) and that they 'generate a kind of moral and character-building spin-off' (*ibid*, p.41). In drawing upon a passage from Caillois (1961) he accepts as a basis for argument that competitive games make winning the 'point of the whole enterprise' (Bailey, 1975, p.40), that the paradigm case for playing games would be playing to win; that the rules are there 'solely to the end of making the claim to have won beyond any dispute' (*ibid*, p.41), in order that players can 'demonstrate their superiority over other individuals or groups' (*ibid*, p.43).

Bailey's objections then to the inclusion of competitive games (sports) in education stems from the fact that he sees competitive games as being tied to the notion of winning. He wants to maintain on account of this that their point lies in beating the opposition in order to demonstrate an unquestioned superiority. What is particularly worrying to Bailey from the 'moral' point of view is that in teaching games 'we are teaching those behaviours and attitudes conducive to the defeat of the other side' (*ibid*). He maintains that 'since winning is the essential objective, then infringements of rules and penalties become a part of the calculation as to whether an action is towards or away from winning' (*ibid*). What is implied here is that the rules of games are merely 'technical and functional and not moral' (*ibid*, p.47). He adds that if competitive games are made *compulsory* this takes us further still from the idea of freedom upon which morality and moral education depends. Bailey concludes from his account of the connection between education and competitive games, especially if they are made compulsory, that we must 'not only abandon the idea that participation in competitive games morally educates, but we must accept the idea that educationally we should seek to diminish, rather than encourage, the importance of competing and winning' (*ibid*, p.48).

On the face of it Bailey's reservations about the place of games in education seem plausible yet a closer examination of them reveals a misunderstanding of what competitive games in the form of rugby, soccer, hockey and cricket and so on are (or should be) all about.

Indeed, he is so committed to the idea of winning as being 'the point of the whole enterprise' that this colours and distorts much else of what he has to say.

To maintain of games, as Bailey does, that winning is *the* point of playing them is to misunderstand why people participate in them. Bailey seems to think that if he can attack and undermine the notion and motive of winning in games he will condemn any worthiness there is in playing them. By concentrating upon the point of winning he not only misconstrues the nature of sporting competition but draws from this a number of questionable conclusions. Comment first of all will be made about Bailey's contention that winning is 'the point of the whole enterprise'.

It would be correct to say that once a game is underway it would not be much of a game if the players did not try to win but it would be quite wrong to assume from this that winning is the sole point of playing them. *Trying to win* then may be considered a necessary feature of competing but this is not to be confused with a person's *reason* or *motive* for playing. For many schoolchildren (as well as for many adults) winning is a prospect rarely achieved but this does not prevent them wanting and continuing to compete and trying to win. Their reason for playing may be to do with fun, fitness, therapy, friendship, sociability, or the pursuit of excellence rather than winning in order to 'demonstrate their superiority over others'.

If as Thompson (1975) points out 'the only point of a competitive game is to win then the only criterion for choosing to play a game is that one's chances of winning are high' (p.150). A person would only participate in those games where this is the case. He would deliberately seek out weak oponents in order to ensure that he won every time. Clearly if this were the case the practice of sport would become absurd. The idea of 'the good contest' or 'the good game' as a reason for competing would cease to exist.[5] What is clear is that although competitive games involve the prospect of producing 'winners' and 'losers', it does not follow that winning is the sole point of playing them. Nor does it follow that their value lies only in being victorious. Weiss (1969), for example, reminds us that:

Even the defeated gain from a game. They benefit from the mere fact that they have engaged in a contest, that they have encountered a display of great skill, that they have made the exhibition of that skill possible or desirable, that they have exerted themselves to the limit, and that they have made a game come to be. (p.183)

Again according to Delattre (1975) it is in moments of test rather than in victory that is the source of value in competition in sport. He writes:

> The testing of one's mettle in competitive athletics is a form of self *discovery* ... The claim of competitive athletics to import-ance rests squarely on their providing us opportunities for self-discovery, for concentration and intensity of involvement, for being carried away by the demands of the contest ... with a frequency seldom matched elsewhere ... This is why it is a far greater success in competitive athletics to have played well under pressure of a truly worthwhile opponent and lost than to have defeated a less worthy or unworthy one where no demands were made. (p.135)

It will be seen then that from the point of view of personal develop-ment more can sometimes be learnt from losing than from winning. The player of games if he is worth his salt, like the politician or business man, has to learn to cope with disappointment as well as with triumph without being unduly affected by either.

By insisting that the only point of playing a game is to win it Bailey rules out any *intrinsic value* it might have. As Dunlop (1975) observes:

> What is logically necessary (for a competitive game to take place) is not necessarily really important in the sense that it must be the 'central' aim of the player or team. (p.156)

What surely above all else the teacher wants to bring about is not a vicious and degenerate form of competitiveness, which is concerned with demonstrating superiority and winning at all costs, but the bringing into being of a 'good game' so that all players can both profit from it and enjoy it. The emphasis here is not on the end result — winning or losing — but rather on *what* takes place and the *manner* in which it takes place. The intelligent use of mastered skills, the well executed tactic, the perceptive employment of strategy, the disciplined blending of team effort are but some of the facets of what makes up the content of a good game. When it comes to the manner in which a game is played a good teacher will be concerned with getting children to understand and willingly abide by the rules, follow their spirit, develop such admired qualities as courage and determination as well as to conduct themselves in a friendly and sportsmanlike way. Trying to win is a part of what it is to have a good game but the result of winning or losing is always subservient to the values inherent in playing a game well. When a game is played well, in the right spirit and the participants learn and derive pleasure from it, neither winning or losing assumes undue importance. When competitive games are played along these lines, as they should be within an educational setting, it will be seen that many perjorative assumptions about the nature of competition disappear. Instead of seeing winning as the point in the playing of games with all the negative undertones this often induces, it becomes possible to see them as human activities, as miniature forms of life, which provide a framework within which physical abilities can be developed and performed, qualities of character fostered and friendly forms of conduct encouraged. A competitive game, as Dearden (1976, p.121) acknowledges, can still be a good one even if one loses. Its value lies in what occurs in the *process* of playing it rather than in its *result*. What seems clear is that the ethos or manner in which a game is seen and approached can be influenced by those who teach it (Meakin, 1952, pp.80–1).

In summary, it has been argued that Bailey's view of competition in relation to games and especially in an educational context, is misconceived. It is misconceived because it fails to appreciate that the historical and normative framework associated with sport is essentially an ethical one. This, of course, is not to say that some of the concerns Bailey expresses are not real ones or that such acts as selfishness, cheating and fouling will not sometimes occur. The point to be refuted here, and the one upon which Bailey rests his case, is that because games are necessarily competitive they are necessarily immoral. It mistakes the idea of competitive sport for certain aspects of abuse that can sometimes occur within it.

The Weak Critique and the Role of the Teacher

Unlike the strong critique, the weak critique does not see competition as inherently wrong but only contingently so. Meakin (1986) writes that:

> The weak critique of competitive sport is that, while not morally wrong in itself, such sport is generally practised in morally undesirable ways. (p.64)

Censure in this case is not so much directed at competition itself but at the abuses which often accompany it. What in effect is being criticized is not competition *per se* but the manner in which it sometimes takes place whether it is to do with violence, intentional rule infringements or generally objectionable ways of behaving. Often, it is said, the young in seeing some of the more unsavory attitudes and habits depicted by their heroes in senior or professional teams come to imitate them, thinking that, even if their behaviour is not praiseworthy, it is the generally expected thing to do.

The problem posed by the weak critique then, is not how to abolish competition because it is thought irredeemably harmful but how to safeguard it from becoming corrupted. The prime question for the school is how to initiate pupils into competitive sports and athletics without them picking up undesirable attitudes and offensive forms of behaviour or, if they do, what can be done about rectifying the situation. Clearly the teacher has an important role to play here. What then can be done to prevent competitive sport becoming a potential source of miseducation or more positively a form of education in which moral values are instantiated? A number of approaches are possible. Three are listed below and each will be considered in turn.

  (i)   altering the value orientation;
 (ii)   making a systematic appeal to rationality;
(iii)   being an exemplar of the ideals to which a commitment has been made. Each of these will be briefly explicated and discussed as to their educational acceptability.

Altering the value orientation

The view of sport that has been previously explicated, which I shall refer to as the traditional view, is one that is best characterized as an ethically-based rule-governed institutionalized social practice marked by competitive whole-bodied but friendly rivalry intrinsic to which is a sense of fair play and sportsmanship. On this view to speak of sport means to speak of competition. The one is a part of the other. Without competition sport would not be what it is. In recent years, however, the phrase 'competitive sport' has been used to connote a 'serious' undertaking of sport in contradistinction to a 'non-serious' or 'recreational' approach. Some educationists, having noted the distinction being made here, have argued that school sport should be designated 'recreational sport' in an effort to detract from its essentially competitive nature. Whilst one can appreciate the motives for a change in orientation it seems to me misguided. Sport, like mathematics or history, is what it is and is not to be confused with whether it is found to be recreative or can be taught in a recreative way. The educational justification for sport forming a part of the movement curriculum is that it is thought to be worthwhile in itself not because it may be found to have recreative value, even though this may be fortuitously the case. This point is not always understood by those who wish to transform the traditional view of sport, which is intrinsically competitive, into something else. If the teacher understands the nature of sport sufficiently well and is committed to it, the Lombardian ethic[6], where winning at all costs is emphasized to the detriment of social and moral values, will not be allowed to develop. What the teacher should be able to control, and condemn, which conversely the professional team manager may sometimes encourage, is the attempt to gain victory by unfair and immoral means.

An equally misguided approach that can be adopted to overcome or prevent sport being practised in undesirable ways is to see it as a means or a vehicle through which social and moral values can be taught and reinforced. Although sport, as has been maintained is inherently concerned with social values and moral qualities, which the teacher may profitably point out relate to life as well as sport, it damages the integrity and educational justification of sport if it is seen and used as but an instrument in the service of the moral educator. The case against this approach towards sport, which largely coincides with what Kew (1978) has called the 'radical ethic'[7], is that it subverts and detracts from sport as being worthwhile in itself.

A similar criticism can be made of what has been called the 'counter culture' approach to sport. In an attempt to overcome the Lombardian ethic, with its overemphasis on winning, it has attempted to promote the idea that 'playing is everything; the end result is unimportant'. In its simplest form Kew (*ibid*) remarks it is 'an approach in which games playing is regarded as pure fun and enjoyment, a love of moving and exercising skill along with other people' (p.109). Again sport is not seen in terms of itself but as a means to something outside itself. This something is not altogether clear but seems to be associated with the notion of authentic existence which is concerned with the 'immediacy of experience, with the here and now, with the process rather than the product' (*ibid*, p.111).

The problem then with all of the above attempts to alter the centrality of competitiveness in sport by orientating it in a different direction, and in so doing reducing it to a form of instrumentalism, is that it no longer remains sport, certainly, at least, in its traditional sense.

Making a systematic appeal to rationality

If, as the traditional view suggests, competitive sport is constituted and governed by rules which logically presuppose fundamental moral principles, such as equality and a respect and concern for the interests of others, what is it that the educationist can do to aid and supplement the process which should be a part of his sportsfield teaching?

Meakin (1981, p.246) suggests that discussion, both formal and informal, should be a part of the teaching process. 'The aim would be to sensitize the developing child to the moral presuppositions of competitive sport and bring home to him that he has some degree of choice whether to abide (by them) or not'. The teacher, he suggests, should not only ask children whether they ought or want to behave in certain ways but, by an appeal to moral reasoning, should condemn 'bad' practices and recommend 'good' ones. Thus, in a rational way, can the development of ethical ideals and modes of conduct such as modesty in victory and dignity in defeat be built up. This, if handled intelligently, could be of assistance in the prevention of anti-social and morally wrong practices, perhaps even in the encouragement and living out of what is demanded by the traditional view of sport. This, however, on its own is not likely to be sufficient. It could, if not related back to sportsfield practice, result in an intellectual acceptance of what is appropriate behaviour without it necessarily occurring. As was intimated earlier being moral is a matter of motivation, character, and conduct as much as reason.

Being an exemplar of the ideals to which a commitment has been made

If, as has been suggested, social and moral conduct in sport, arises not so much from understanding the rules and the principles upon which they are based but in the dispositions and attitudes cultivated and practised, it follows that rational discussion, whilst helpful, is on its own not sufficient. What perhaps is needed in the sphere of sport, no less than other areas of the curriculum, is that pupils perceive what is required of them. If children are able to see what it is to act honestly, fairly, bravely, resolutely and generously whilst in competition they are more likely to be impressed by such acts than by a discussion of them.

Rationality, then, is one thing but manifestations of virtue are another. Acts of sportsmanship are more likely to fire the imagination and do more for the ideals of sport than any amount of casuistry. That is why it is important that the teacher, the guardian of the best traditions of sport, should be conscious of his role for it is he who sets the standards that those in his care are likely to follow. He should understand that how to conduct oneself on the sportsfield is likely to be as much caught as taught. It is not enough then, that the teacher be a clear interpreter of the rules of sport. What is required in addition is to show himself as being genuinely committed to the forms of consideration and conduct it demands. It is unlikely that social and moral values in sport can be effectively taught unless the teacher shows a commitment to such values himself. This is, of course, a tall order yet it is not an impossible one to fulfil. It is because of the power of example and commitment that it becomes all the more necessary in the words of Warnock (1977) 'for teachers to know what they are at, what characteristics they are displaying, since their virtues and vices will form a part of the whole picture of possible moral behaviour that a child will, gradually, build up' (pp.135–6).

In being conscious of their role, however, it is as well for them to remember Ryle's (1975) comment that:

> ... in matters of morality as distinct from techniques, good examples had better not be set with edifying purpose. (p.57)

The point here is that if the teacher is too intent or heavy-handed in the presentation of himself as a model, or is seen not to be genuine, he is likely to be scorned, ridiculed or perhaps even worse, disregarded.

What in the last resort a sports' teacher's work is measured by is not so much in the moral educatedness of his pupils' dispassionate judgments but in terms of their attitudes and conduct as they engage in the fervour and challenge of competition.

Notes

1   Fielding (1976) writes:

> An 'essentially contested' concept is one about which disputes do not resolve themselves even when the contestants are aware of rival interpretations. Indeed, disputants seek to establish further arguments and justifications to back up their claims in order to establish even more firmly their own particular interpretation. In this kind of situation some philosophers have tended to take the view that the issues are resolvable and that resolution is likely to be brought about by examining the metaphysical presuppositions of the participants. (p.135)

However, W B Gallie (1956), who first coined the notion of an essentially contested concept, suggests that, although endless disputes do remain endless precisely because of metaphysical or indeed psychological recalcitrance, this need not necessarily be the case. With certain concepts that are central to aesthetics, political philosophy and philosophy of religion these apparently endless disputes

> are perfectly genuine: (and) although not resolvable by argument of any kind, are nevertheless sustained by perfectly respectable argument and evidence ... These mutually contesting, mutually contested uses of the concept (make) up its standard general use. (p.169)

2 Fielding (1976 pp.126–9) cites as omissions: the relationship between competition and regulation; the nature of the regulation; whether competition is object-centred or opponent-centred; whether it is voluntary or involuntary; whether reference is being made to the competitive process or the competitive motive.

3 Simon (1985), for example, writes that competition in the context of sports can be defended on the grounds that it is 'a mutually acceptable quest for excellence' (p.28).

4 Although Bailey's (1975) article refers to games he is really talking about those competitive activities called sports. For the purpose of this section I have left his terminology as it is.

5 Comments by Arnold and Fraleigh are of interest here. Fraleigh (1984, chapters 8 and 9) writes that the good contest shall be in part characterized by such ethical considerations as equal opportunities for optimal performance, non-injurious action, non-harassment courtesy and sympathetic regard. Arnold (1979) refers to the 'good contest' as having three separate but interrelated aspects — 'the good strife, the creation and discharge of enjoyable tension and the aesthetic living out of skills and strategies' (p.161).

6 The Lombardian ethic is so called because it derives from a famous American football coach Vince Lombardi who is reported to have said 'winning is not the most important thing; it's the only thing'.

It is of interest to note that what Lombardi is claimed to have actually said is 'winning isn't everything, but wanting to win is' (see Morris, 1979).

7 The radical ethic is perhaps best exemplified by the English public schools of the mid-nineteeth century which used sports as a means of social and moral reinforcement (see Kew, 1978, p.104).

6   Aesthetic Education and the Nature of Physical Activities

It will be recalled that although the initiation view of education recognizes aesthetics as a form of knowledge it says, relatively speaking, little about it. Insofar as it is explicated it tends to be in terms of *artistic* knowledge rather than with aesthetic activity or experience. Hirst, for example, (1974) writes:

> In seeking to characterize works of art, paintings, poems symphonies etc, as artistic statements, parallel to scientific statements or, say, mathematical statements, historical statements or moral statements, I am concerned with the artistic knowledge they express and can communicate ... (p.153)

The thrust of his 'propositional theory of art', which is his main concern in discussing aesthetics, is that he sees works such as *Guernica, Middlemarch* or *Fidelio* as symbolic expressions which have meaning and which, like sentences, make statements about the everyday world. Like other forms of statement he maintains they can be found true or false. Whether or not it is misleading to think of the arts in terms of 'statement-making' propositions, however, is not the present concern. Rather it is to note, before commenting on it, that Hirst's approach to aesthetics is one of criticism and judgment in literature and the fine arts and not with aesthetic activity or the nature of aesthetic experience.

White (1973, pp.25–31), another exponent of the initiation view of education, also seems to see aesthetic education predominantly in terms of theory rather than of practice. He suggests that aesthetic *appreciation* should be compulsory for all pupils whereas *engagement in art-marking activities* should only be voluntary. Not only is White here revealing an intellectual bias but in effect is ensuring that *some* pupils would never, as a part of their formal education, obtain any practical experience or be provided with opportunities for creative endeavour at all. By relegating practical and/or creative activities to the status of voluntary activities White clearly thinks that the basis of aesthetic education lies in what he calls the 'comtemplative mode' rather than in active engagement. Indeed he seems to want to place at the forefront of aesthetic education, as does Hirst, an understanding and evaluation of works of art by means of criteria marked out by such terms as 'beautiful', 'elegant', 'graceful', 'exquisite', 'ugly', 'gauche', 'clumsy', 'garish' and so on as if this in itself is somehow constitutive of an aesthetic education[1]. Suffice it to say for the moment I find this approach to aesthetic education as limiting as it is biased.

Perhaps enough has been said to suggest that aesthetic education involves more than a study of art and the learning of appropriate concepts in order to discuss, appreciate and evaluate it. As I have pointed out elsewhere[2] if the notion of education as initiation means anything it is surely to do with getting young people to actually engage in such activities as painting, dancing, acting, singing, playing instruments and composing rather than just commenting upon or learning how to appreciate the great works of others. Important though the correct application of concepts is to aesthetic appraisal and art criticism it is surely the first task of the school to get children to be able to participate in aesthetic activities rather than judge them. By knowing how to participate, by getting to know an activity from the 'inside', the child will, with good teaching, become more discerning about his own work as well as that of others. It is surely preferable that at school aesthetic evaluation, a necessary element in aesthetic education, should stem primarily from the struggle to improve practice rather than from a detached study of masterpieces from the present or past. This, of course, is neither to denigrate nor to deny the value of aesthetic appreciation. Clearly trips to the concert hall, art gallery, or theatre can be insightful occasions. Even so, discourse *about* art, important though it is to aesthetic understanding, is by no means a sufficient condition for an aesthetic education. There is a difference as Collinson (1973) points out between *aesthetic involvement* and *aesthetic commentating*. She observes:

> The aesthetically educated person is not so much the person who is able to talk about, describe or *comment* upon certain objects and situations in a certain way, as the person who in fact has a capacity for experiencing, understanding and becoming *involved* with them ... (p.197)

Whereas aethetic commentating may be regarded as an ability to make certain sorts of remarks about a work of art without necessarily being moved by it, aesthetic involvement is more concerned with being taken up by it; of being absorbed and entranced by its aesthetic appeal. Our consciousness, as Collinson (*ibid*) puts it, is 'wholly pervaded and informed by the object' (p.203). It is possible, as Elliott (1972) makes clear, to be a lover of art as well as a critic of it. They are essentially two different perspectives. Whereas the critic is primarily concerned with looking *at* the objective features of a work of art and commentating upon them with a view to making some kind of detached assessment of it, the lover, on the other hand, is concerned more with entering *into* a sympathetic and imaginative relationship with it. He will be more concerned with leaving himself open to the experience it has the power to evoke, than intellectually appraising its good and bad points.

What both the above writers want to emphasize is that aesthetic education should be concerned as much with the provision of aesthetic experience, in so far as this can be done, as with criticism and the mastery of appropriate aesthetic terminology.

Both viewpoints, it can perhaps be agreed, are important. If they are left separate and hostile, rather than complementary and mutually enriching, the nature and purpose of aesthetic education will be impoverished.

Lest the observations above concerning 'commentary' and 'involvement' should be miscontrued in terms of 'reason' on the one hand and 'feeling' on the other, it should be pointed out that insofar as aesthetic education involves an education of the emotions there is, or need be no incompatibility, for as both Peters (1975) and Hepburn (1975) argue, emotions are forms of cognition. To feel fear, for example, is to see a situation as dangerous; to feel envious is to see someone else as possessing something I want. What emotions have in common is the fact that they involve appraisals of one sort or another. To see somebody, a situation, a quality 'as' something, is to perceive it and evaluate it, rightly or wrongly, in a particular way. What is 'seen' is logically related to how we 'feel' about it. What follows from this is that if our perception of something changes so our feeling towards it also tends to change. To have the purpose and significance of a dance explained so that it is more completely understood is to have our perception of it altered and with it our emotional response. The point then is that if aesthetic education is centrally, if not exclusively, concerned with the enlargement of emotional experience and the vitality of affective life, it is very much connected to cognition and how things are perceived and understood. In this respect 'cognition', which is heavily dependent on language, and 'feeling' are complementary and by no means disparate[3]. It is the ability of the teacher to give reasons about how a work of art or situation is or can be understood and responded to, that makes an education in the arts and other aspects of aesthetic life possible.

Perhaps enough has been said to suggest that in schools aesthetic education should be concerned firstly with the teaching of aesthetic practices so that pupils learn how to engage in them. In the practice of them pupils will, with good teaching, learn to move from where they are as Reid (1979) puts it 'towards something more discriminating, finer, richer, fuller, more complex' (p.81). Secondly, pupils should be taught in such a way that the possibility for aesthetic involvement and experience is encouraged. In this respect much depends not only on what is planned for but also upon the environment and general teaching climate. Thirdly, aesthetic concepts, when introduced, should be developed and used so that not only the work of others can be better appreciated but more particularly that their own activities can be practised and expressed with greater knowledge and understanding.

On this last point Redfern (1986) writes:

> aesthetic education consists centrally in the cultivating of an individual's capacity to regard things, including things which he himself might have made or be making or performing, with a particular kind of imaginative attention and to become increasingly discriminating and critically reflective in his responses to them. (p.67)

Having criticized an over intellectualistic approach to aesthetic education and suggested a more balanced and practical one, it is proposed now to look at movement activities in relation to the aesthetic so that it can be more clearly ascertained than is customarily the case which of them, logically speaking, has the greatest aesthetic potential as far as teaching and learning is concerned. Before doing this, however, it will be helpful, in order to dispel possible confusion later, to differentiate between the aesthetic and art.

The Aesthetic and Art

It is normally recognized that the notion of the aesthetic is wider than that of art. Yet with many writers this distinction is often disregarded. The elision of one with the other can lead to considerable confusion. It is sometimes said, for example, by physical educationists who are seeking to find an acceptable educational argument for the inclusion of physical activities in the curriculum, that because physical activities can be seen in an aesthetic way that this in itself provides a justification for them having a place[4]. Alternatively, and perhaps somewhat more strangely, it is sometimes claimed that sport is a form of art and because art is considered educationally respectable then *ipso facto* so too should sport be[5].

In view of these blanket and ill-considered claims it will be helpful to make some brief preliminary remarks about the aesthetic in relation to art in order to help clear the ground for what is to follow.

It can be said that an aesthetic situation develops whenever an *aesthetic attitude* is adopted, or evoked towards an object and is entered into for no other reason than the enjoyment it affords. It differs from that of the *practical attitude* where things tend to be seen in instrumental terms. Thus, if a diamond necklace, for example, is seen only in terms of its commercial viability or as a gift in order to pacify one's wife the attitude adopted would be practical rather than aesthetic. That is to say, instead of the necklace being perceived in an aesthetic way it is seen rather as means towards some other end.

The aesthetic attitude is sometimes referred to as being a distinctive mode of consciousness; a particular way of perceiving something. Stolnitz (1960) speaks of it as a form of:

> distinterested and sympathetic attention to and contemplation of any object of awareness whatever, for its own sake alone.
> (p.35)

The aesthetic then is a concept which refers to the possibility of perceiving things from a particular point of view. Mass-produced objects such as washing machines or stamps, hand-made objects such as chairs or drinking mugs, natural objects such as sunsets or mountain peaks, and objets trouvé such as a stone or piece of driftwood, are all possible objects of aesthetic perception, as well as those objects which are normally considered art objects.

Aesthetic perception, it should be noted, always takes on an *object* (the aesthetic object) but it should be made clear that the aesthetic is not necessarily confined to the visual. It relates to all modes of perception — to taste, touch, sound, smell and not least the kinaesthetic. The taste of wine, the touch of silk, the sound of music, the smell of fresh cut hay, the feel of a tennis serve or the motion of scything, are all possible aesthetic 'objects' and all are capable of yielding aesthetic satisfaction. It will be seen then that the aesthetic in life is open and almost boundless. It is not, as is sometimes implied, confined to a particular type of context or a particular kind or recherché sensibility.

What then has been said is that when objects are perceived aesthetically they are perceived in a *particular way for their own sake*. To put the point another way when an object is perceived aesthetically it carries its own intrinsic satisfaction or reward regardless of its functional or utilitarian value.

What then of art? Art is important in the realm of the aesthetic in that its objects are often considered paradigm cases of the aesthetic. Art objects, it is sometimes said, are attempts to exemplify the aesthetic. The arts of painting, sculpture, dance and drama are distinctive in that they are imaginative creations of man that are *intended* to be objects of aesthetic delight and/or aesthetic appreciation. Beardsley (1979) for example, writes that an artwork can be defined 'as an intentional arrangement of conditions for affording experiences with marked aesthetic character'. (p.729)

Despite such attempts to get at the meaning of art it is now generally recognized that art is an open concept. That is to say, no single theory has yet been formulated or set of necessary and sufficient conditions produced to accommodate the varied ways in which the term is used. Weitz (1970. pp.177–8), in recognizing the adventurous and everchanging character of art, suggests that it is likely to remain impossible to explain its meaning by referring to any one set of defining properties. Nonetheless, it is helpful to point to the descriptive and evaluative senses in which it is used. Thus, it is not uncommon that when 'we *describe* something as a work of art, we do so under conditions of there being present some sort of artifact, made by human skill, ingenuity, and imagination, which embodies its sensuous public medium — stone, wood, sound, words etc — certain distinquishable elements and relations'. On the other hand, when an artifact is *evaluated* as an art object it is perceived and judged according to aesthetic criteria. The question then arises as to what counts as 'aesthetic' criteria. The answer to this is often found to be dependent upon which aesthetic theory is particularly favoured. Thus, for formalists a painting may be appraised predominantly in terms of its 'significant form' or the particular arrangement of its lines, colour, shapes and so on. For emotionalists it would be looked at predominantly from the point of view of its expressive power. What makes the various theories of art valuable is not that they have provided a universal agreement about what art means but rather that they have yielded important insights about its nature whether these are to do with 'form', 'emotional impact' or the unique presentation of a particular kind of truth. Reasons for excellence in art are not confined to any one theoretical construct of it.

What it is necessary to realized about art is that it is not removed or detached from life but grows out of it and plays back into it. The emotions expressed in art, for example, could not be understood without understanding the emotions of people in everyday life. They could not be intelligibly evoked, in other words, unless they had something in common with the contexts of life from which they come. It is because of this that art is able sometimes to encapsulate societal issues which are of social, moral or political significance. One example of this last kind is found in Jooss's *Green Table* where the ineptitude and posturing of statesman before the Second World War is parodied with delicious irony. As Best (1985) puts it 'in the arts, the notions of learning, understanding and experience cannot intelligibly be regarded as distinct from learning, understanding and experience in life situations generally' (pp.163-4).

Finally, it is perhaps necessary to emphasize that although what is designated art can be described, interpreted and evaluated it does not and cannot necessarily guarantee the provision of *aesthetic experience* ie. the experience rendered possible while the aesthetic attitude is being sustained. Conversely, it should be understood that just because an object is found to be aesthetic, interesting or rewarding in some way it does not necessarily suggest that it is art. Both these points should be borne in mind in the sections that follow.

The Aesthetic and the Logic of Physical Activities

When physical activities are carefully examined in relation to the aesthetic it is possible to divide them up into three logically separate categories: (i) those sports that are non-aesthetic; (ii) those sports that are partially aesthetic; and (iii) those activities such as dance and mime that can be considered art. In order to explicate what is suggested I propose to look firstly at sport, and secondly at dance.

Sport and the Aesthetic

In an effort to clear up some of the confusions endemic in the literature to do with aesthetics and sport Best (1978) made a distinction between 'purposive' sport and 'aesthetic' sports (pp.99–122). *Purposive sports*, he maintains, are characterized by the fact that each of these sports can be specified independently of the manner of achieving it, as long as it conforms to the rules or norms which govern it. Included in the category of purposive sports are those like football, rugby, hockey, track and field, basketball, baseball and tennis. The point about them is that the aesthetic is not intrinsic to their purpose which is to win by scoring the most goals, tries, baskets, points, runs; or the recording of the best times and distances and so on. The point is a logical one. An activity like handball would still count as handball even if there was no reference to, or concern for, the aesthetic at all. This is not to deny that such sports can still be considered from the aesthetic point of view. It means rather that they are not inherently concerned with the aesthetic. They can and do provide from time to time, either by accident or design, aesthetic moments but these are not *necessarily* or logically a part of their purpose. *Aesthetic sports*, on the other hand, are so called because 'the aim cannot intelligibly be specified independently of the means of achieving it' (*ibid*, p 105). Included in this smaller category are such activities as gymnastics, diving, skating, synchronized swimming, trampolining, ski jumping and surfing. Inherent in all these sports is a concern for the way or manner in which they are performed. How they are done is a part or purpose of the activity. It is not accidental or fortuitous but a necessary feature of what that activity is. It helps define the nature and character of what is being done. The Olympic gymnast, for example, whose *only* concern was to perform her routine on the horizontal bars without reference to the *manner* in which she performed would have misconceived the purpose of the activity. As one reference (White, 1966) on gymnastics states:

> A perfect exercise with a maximum rating is one that is presented with elegance, ease, precision and in a style and rhythm well adapted to the nature of the aesthetic performance with no faults in execution. The faults in execution or style are penalized by a deduction in points or fraction of points according to the following direction.
>
> Defects in elegance in general. An exercise, although executed without fault, but presented in a rhythm too quick or too slow, or with an ill-proportioned display of force, counts less than a perfect exercise as described ... (p.61)

Similarly in skating marks are awarded for 'artistic grace' as well as 'technical merit'. Among the terms used on this former component are 'harmonious composition', 'conformity with the music', and 'carriage'. What above all should be achieved is a movement that is 'effortless, flowing and graceful' (ISU, 1973–75, p.61). An example of the way in which gymnastics can be aesthetically perceived by a knowledgeable onlooker (Curl, 1980) is conveyed by the following description:

> Her (Ludmilla Tourischeva) sequence was above all expressive, with a medley of qualities from nonchalance, playful arrogance ... coyness and at times piquancy. Even dramatic qualities emerged with climax, tension, resolution, but perhaps dominantly characteristic was her lyricism, rhythmicality, and closely integrated movements with the accellorandos, rubatos and rallentandos with the music.

What marks out the aesthetic sport is that its purpose can only be specified in terms of the aesthetic manner of achieving it. Put the other way round *the aesthetic sport is one in which the purpose cannot be specified without reference to the aesthetic manner of achieving it.*

Before proceeding to the third category perhaps some general comments on what has so far been said would be helpful. Best's distinction between some sports and others with regard to their aesthetic content is valid and useful. To characterize this distinction, however, in terms of the difference between 'purposive' sports and 'aesthetic' ones is somewhat misleading. It suggests that aesthetic sports are 'non-purposive' and this is clearly not the case. The chief difficulty here is with the word 'purposive'. What this means is unclear. Does Best mean that purposive sports are explained by the goal or result aimed at which he suggests is winning? Surely not, for if this were the case 'aesthetic sports' would be found equally purposeful for they too are concerned with winning. They differ only in that the aesthetic is a part of the requirement of winning. If this is the case, as it seems to be, it is perfectly legitimate to say that both categories are purposive but whereas activities in his first group (purposive sports) are concerned only with winning within the rules those in his second group (aesthetic sports) are not just concerned with winning within the rules but with winning within the rules a part of which are concerned with the giving of aesthetic guidance. What follows from this is that it is more intelligible, it seems to me, to speak of 'non-aesthetic' sports and ones which are 'partially aesthetic'. Nonetheless even if this modified rendering of Best's position is accepted there is the further implication in his writings, especially when he is writing of 'purposive sports', that sport exists for the sake of winning as if this were its only purpose. If this is the case, as it seems to be, then further comment is required. As I pointed out earlier there is a distinction between regarding a sport as an activity which has as its only concern *winning*, and regarding it as an activity which, amongst other things, is concerned with *trying to win*. No sport, it is being suggested, has as its sole purpose the end *result* of winning but it does have the inbuilt *procedural expectation* that contestants should, within the rules, try to win. 'Purpose' in sport is not to be confused with or taken as being commensurate with the logical but trivial point of winning; nor even with trying to win. Rather it is bound up with a complex network of beliefs, attitudes, values, customs and rules which, together, make up a miniature form of life in which participants find purpose. Put another way each separate sport has its own distinctive purpose and this is to a large extent bound up with the rules which help characterize it as being the one that it is. Each sport then can be regarded as having a purpose of its own and some sports as we have seen have as a part of their purpose an inherent concern for the aesthetic; others do not. To categorize only some sports as having purpose, with the implication that others do not, is therefore as unfortunate as it is misleading.

Dance and the Aesthetic

As was made clear earlier, to speak of the aesthetic is not necessarily to speak of art yet, as has been shown, it is not unusual to think of art as a paradigm case of the aesthetic. In speaking of some physical activities as art it is possible to think in terms of a third logical category of movement in relation to the aesthetic – *'the artistic category'*. Here I am thinking in particular of the activities of dance (as an art form) and mime. Such activities are characterized by the fact that the purpose of art is art itself. In art there is no gap between *what* is done and the *manner* in which it is done. Another way to put this is to say that there is no separation between the nature of the activity and its mode of presentation. Artistic activities, by their very make-up, are intrinsically concerned with aesthetic considerations. This is their *raison d'etre*. What gives a work of art its distinctive character is that there is an inseparable fusion of form and content. In music (for example, in a Bach fugue) this inseparability perhaps becomes most strikingly evident. In a sense the form is the content. All art, it has been said, aspires to this condition of 'oneness'. To speak of ends and means in art is misconceived for, as in education, the means are in part the ends. Just as in education the *moral manner* in which things are taught is as important as *what* is done so in art the *aesthetic form* is as important as the *content*. What marks out a work of art, perhaps above all else, is that its meaning cannot be expressed in any way other than the way it is. It is this fact about a work of art that makes it *sui generis*. To put the matter another way a work of art is a unique presentation of embodied meaning. In it content and form are fused into a single entity. In the movement art forms of dance and mime the phrase embodied meaning is particularly apt for what is aesthetically achieved is done through the medium of the actions of the embodied person[6]. In dance although the art form, the *object d'art* is the dance and not the dancer, there is an important sense in which the dancer is the dance. It is only by the dancer being able to become the dance by embodying and projecting the sensory, formal and expressive qualities intended by the choreographer that he or she is able to communicate the dance as being aesthetically meaningful. It is of interest then that Friesen (1975) in writing of the perception of dance observes:

> The dancer must ... remain one with the dance to preserve
> the unity and continuity of the aesthetic image. The technical
> competence of the dancer includes not only the physical skills
> required to perform the dance, but the ability to exist within
> the dynamic illusion of the dance. (p.101)

It will be seen that the difference between *partially aesthetic* physical activities, such as gymnastics, and those which *are artistic activities*, such as dance, is that whereas in the former the gap between their purpose and the aesthetic is never entirely closed, (ie their purpose could still to some extent be fulfilled in the absence of the aesthetic,) in the latter it would be logically misconceived to think in terms of a gap at all. Another way to put this is to say that the purpose of art lies in the aesthetic, ie, it lies in the creation of a significant aesthetic object which is its purpose. Talk, therefore, between ends and means in art is singularly inappropriate for they cannot be independently specified: they are in an important sense one and the same. In artistic activities, like dance and mime, aesthetic qualities, whether formal or expressive, are not there merely by accident, nor are they just called upon to demonstrate a qualitative distinction between one type of performance and another. They are there because in an indispensibly central way they help characterize and constitute the very nature of the activity. It is for this reason they are important activities in movement and aesthetic education.

In common with other arts, dance has features that distinguish it as being an 'art object'. It deliberately sets out to evoke an aesthetic, as opposed to a utilitarian, response in the spectator. 'Its fundamental office' in the words of Phenix (1970, p.10) 'is to create in the perci-pient a significant emotion, valuable in itself, and not merely to serve as an instrument of some other purpose'. Each dance is a unique composition, expressing its own immanent structure and as such is subject only to its own inherent demands. For both dancer and specta-tor each dance requires an imaginative response that is not governed or unduly influenced by what has been done or witnessed before.

As an art, dance 'calculates' its display of aesthetic qualities and it is the dancer who does his or her best to express them. What is done, difficult and technical though it may be, is intrinsic to the creation of an artisitic performance. Any self-indulgence or over-statement is likely to result in distorting and weakening the very effect that is intended. The discipline of the dancer is imposed by the medium of the dance itself. Each dance develops its own unique form and struc-ture and becomes an independent, free and separate entity at the centre of which is the embodied dancing person.

The Perspective of the Performer in Contrast to That of the Spectator

In looking into the spectrum of physical activities that make up the movement curriculum it has been shown that some activities are more inherently concerned with the aesthetic than others. It should be clear therefore, at least from the logical point of view, that activities such as dance and mime offer more scope in terms of aesthetic education than activities like rugby and soccer. They are, after all, *intrinsically* con-cerned with the aesthetic and permit the teacher to enlarge a pupil's aesthetic awareness as a result of the concepts, qualities they entail, as well as the emotions and feelings with which they are frequently associated. Nonetheless, as was suggested earlier, the aesthetic and the possibility of aesthetic experience is by no means confined to the arts. It can and frequently does occur in what I have called for purposes of analysis, 'non-aesthetic' activities as well as with 'partially aesthetic' or 'artistic' ones. It is because movement as a source of aesthetic experi-ence has not, especially in educational circles, been extensively ex-plored or very much written about, that I propose explicating its potential even if this is seen to be only in a peripheral or incidental way.

In order to bring out in a distinctive way the aesthetic potential of sport in as full a manner as possible, the perspective of the performer will be taken in contrast to that of the spectator. By so doing it is hoped to identify some aspects of aesthetic perception and experience that would otherwise remain undisclosed.

In highlighting, however, the differences between the perspective of the participant *in* sport in contrast to that of the observer *of* sport, it must readily be understood that there is a good deal of 'overlap' between the two stances. Both, for example, understand that each and every sport has its own set of rules which help characterize and govern it. Both too, will realize that each sport has its own traditions, customs and conventions which help mark it out as being the one it is. The knowledgeable performer and spectator alike, understand that each sport takes place within a context in which certain skills, tactics and strategies are part and parcel of what constitutes the nature of that sport. Such understandings and agreements form the basis of what is held in common about sport, regardless of whether one is looking *at* it or taking part *in* it. Such understandings, it can be said, are a part of our inter-subjective or common 'form of life'[7]. Without it there would be no communication, no meaningful sharing of experience.

While it is obvious that a good deal of 'common ground' exists between the standpoint of the performer and that of the spectator when considering the aesthetic in sport, it should not be overlooked that there are also a number of important differences.

The first is that the performer is a participant and takes his or her perspective from '*inside*' the activity in which he or she is engaged. The spectator, on the other hand, looks upon the activity as a witness, so to speak, from the 'outside'. Whilst the performer is in and of the action, or '*involved*' as Curl (1976, p.51) puts it, the spectator is, relatively speaking, remove or '*detached*' and physically apart from it.

Second, whilst the performer or participant is author and agent of his or her own actions and in the words of Beck (1975) 'knows what he is doing in the sense of what he means to accomplish' (p.45), the spectator or onlooker remains basically a reader or interpreter of what he sees. Given the context, or 'common ground' of the action, the spectator is able to make certain inferences about the performer's intentions but these cannot be taken for granted as being the same.

Third, the performer in action is able (this is not to say that he always does or should) to attend to his own lived-body experiences and constitute them as meaningful. As agent, for example, I am able, (if I so choose) to attend to my own kinaesthetic flow patterns as I engage in particular forms of contextual movement actions. As I do, so I am able to 'feel'. *What* I feel, in this sense, logically arises from my direct acquaintance of knowing how to do things. Only a knowledgeable performer (or knowledgeable ex-performer) can have (or can have had) such feelings[8].

Fourth, for the spectator, 'qualitative movement' in sport, tends to be 'seen' rather than 'felt'. For the spectator the aesthetic perception of sport is predominantly of a visual order. It is witnessed and appraised in terms of such well-established criteria a 'rhythm', 'symmetry' or 'harmony'. Whereas for the performer in such sports as ice-dancing or synchronized swimming, for example, aesthetic qualities like 'balance', 'continuity', 'proportion', 'unity', 'repetition' and 'contrast', are physically expressed and experienced, for the spectator they offer essentially only visual delight. What characterizes what might be called the 'performer's aesthetic' from that of the spectator's is that it involves an experienced expressive act. For the performer aesthetic perception lies in the performance of the action[9] for the spectator it lies more in its appreciative observation.

What I have tried to show is that despite a considerable 'common ground' that exists between the perspective of the performer and that of the spectator, there are also some important differences. I am suggesting that when it comes to the aesthetic perception and experience of sport these differences constitute the basis of what are two essentially different stances[10].

In order to explicate more fully what the stance of the performer is and how it differs from that of the spectator, I propose now to discuss briefly four themes. These are: the performer as the embodiment of aesthetic and expressive qualities; the performer as one who seeks the acquisition and mastery of skills; the performer as the incarnate location of identifiable and distinctive kinaesthetic flow patterns; and lastly, the performer as actor in search of 'the good contest' and 'the well-played game'.

The Performer's Aesthetic : Four Themes

Writers like Lowe (1977) and Fisher (1972) have made it abundantly clear that the aesthetic and the beautiful are frequently contingent upon the practice of sport, as when for example, the mountaineer is able to glory in the splendour of his surroundings; or when the surfer is able to rejoice in the rhythmic sound of waves. Fascinating though this aspect of the aesthetic is in relation to sport, comment here will be confined to the nature and actions of sport itself.

*The Performer as the Embodiment of Aesthetic and
Expressive Qualities*

It has been suggested that the aesthetic perception of sport for the
spectator is predominantly a visual matter. It consists largely in being
able to pick out, from what is presented, qualities which can be
appreciated for what they are. For the spectator the aesthetic experience of sport arises predominantly from being able to recognize aesthetic qualities and react to them in an appropriate way. As Reimer
(1970) observes:

> To the extent that a person can perceive aesthetic qualities
> keenly, subtly, precisely, sophisticatedly, sensitively, his re-
> action can be keen, subtle, precise, sophisticated, sensitive.
> (p. 82)

Although in a highly aesthetic sport, such as ice dancing, aesthetic
qualities are presented for the spectator to behold and appreciate, it
is from the performer's perspective, more a question of how best to
present and display them in order that they can be appreciated. It
is the task of the skater, for example, to be a source and vehicle of
beauty. In skating the skater must become the embodiment of form
and feeling. It is in the successful fusion of form with feeling that
his or her own aesthetic gratification lies.[11] The skater is both able to
articulate and express aesthetic qualities and at the same time derive
aesthetic pleasure from so doing. If for the spectator aesthetic meaning
derives mostly from the *product* presented, for the skater it derives
mostly from the *process* of doing. The ice dancer is able to experience
himself as the personification of expressive form. As Arnold (1979b)
has observed:

> In the harmonious blending of *motion* with *emotion* the dancer
> is able to realize himself as few others have the power to do.
> What is felt and meaningfully constituted, although sometimes
> capable of being described in words, is not reducible to words.
> Its 'meaningfulness' lies in its own mode of expression. (p. 143)

The Performer as one who Seeks the Mastery of Skills

Related to the question of the performer as the embodiment of aesthetic and expressive quality is the question of the acquisition and mas-

tery of skills. Without the acquisition of techniques and skills sport would not fulfil its own possibility either for the spectator or the performer.

Skills in sport not only help characterize and mark out one sport from another, but may also be regarded as indispensible exemplifications of 'knowing how' to take part. Just as soccer requires the ability to dribble, trap and pass, tennis requires the ability to serve, volley and lob. Such skills have to be worked for and achieved. When mastered they may be looked upon as particular instances of practical knowledge, whereby what the performer does in a rule-governed context, is seen to be intelligent and competent. Put another way, practical knowledge, or 'knowing how', is essentially to do with the mastery of skills and being able to perform them successfully with understanding. In the mastery of techniques and skills the performer strives for a particular kind of perfection.

What is being suggested is that each sport, partially through the skills that help define and characterize it, has its own limitations and possibilities for personal expression and experience. One of the paradoxes of participating in sport is that it is necessary to be disciplined in order to be free, not only to express but to experience. As Farson (1978) observes, techniques 'make genuinely expressive experience possible (p.14). To put the same point somewhat differently, I am maintaining that the practice of a sport involves its own set of techniques and skills and that these largely constitute the ways and means of the possibility of individual achievement and experience.

It would, or course, be wrong to assume that because a sport is practised skilfully it is necessarily aesthetic but many skills do, because of their easy, smooth, rhythmical nature, invite aesthetic attention. Stolnitz (1973) is one of the few aestheticians who recognizes not only that:

> Outside the arts, there is a large class of actions, appropriately described as skilful, which when thus described, has good claim to be counted aesthetic,

but also that:

> ... the skilful so far from falling outside and being contingently related to the aesthetic is itself a major sector of the aesthetic. (p.7)

Curl, (1976, p.47) rightly points out, that the highly skilled performer becomes the possessor of a new and expanded range of perceptions. In what Slusher (1967, p.79) has called the 'personification of perfection' (p.179), the performer is able sometimes to enter into a state of what can only be described as 'aesthetic being'. In speaking of archery, for example, Herrigell (1971) observes that:

> After right shots the breath glides effortlessly to its end, whereupon air is unhurriedly breathed in again. The heart continues to beat evenly and quietly, and with concentration undisturbed one can go on to the next shot. But inwardly, for the archer himself, right shots have the effects of making him feel the day has just begun. He feels in a mood for all right doing, and, what is even more important, for not doing. Delectable indeed is this state. (p.78)

The Performer as the Incarnate Location of Identifiable and Distinctive Kinaesthetic Flow Patterns

If there are relatively few references to the performer's perspective in relation to sport, there are fewer still, in relation to the performer's kinaesthetic experiences[12]. This is surprising, for it is not uncommon amongst sportsmen and dancers, that as performers they are sometimes able to appreciate kinaesthetically what it is that they are doing.

The aesthetic perception of kinaesthetic feelings, or 'kine-aesthetic' perception, is most likely to occur when skills as patterns of motion have been mastered. It should be emphasized that kinaesthetic perception should not be confused with vague, undifferentiated sensations but should be understood in terms of clear, distinctively and sensitively felt, flow patterns which arise from and accompany skilled movements. Put another way they are, paradigmatically, the feeling of which I am, or can be, aware and take pleasure in, when I 'kine-aesthetically' perceive an action as a result of 'knowing how to perform it. Kine-aesthetic feelings, in other words, are most knowingly felt and appreciated when they are most skilfully performed and especially when there is time and inclination to dwell upon them. Hence some sports, and the skills that help characterize them are likely to yield more ' kine-aesthetic' gratification than others. In sculling, for example, where the oarsman is caught up in the regular, rhythms of gliding, stretching and pulling there is time to take pleasure in the motions themselves. It is therefore not surprising that Dietz speaks of 'that tremendous feeling of moving across the water'.[13]

If for the spectator aesthetic satisfaction derives from seeing a well-balanced, poised and disciplined rowing eight, working in unison, it falls to the crew to kine-aesthectically feel the rhythmical unity and power that flows from their harmonious efforts.[14]

Although not all sports are like rowing in that they provide such a sustained opportunity for kine-aesthetic experience, others are not devoid of this possibility, though it may come more fleetingly. In the cadence of the tennis serve, the swimmer's tumble turn, the javelin thrower's delivery, the gymnast's floor sequence, the agent as performer is able 'feelingly' to know what action is being performed and derive kine-aesthetic satisfaction while doing it.

The Performer as Actor in Search of 'the Good Contest' and 'the Well-played Game'

Sport is not drama, yet as Keenan (1973, pp.309–26) has shown, it is possible to look upon it *as if* it were. To say that sport is not drama, however, is not to say that it cannot be at times dramatic or spectacular; nor does it mean that the player cannot or does not see himself as a sort of actor in which he takes a craftsmanlike pride in his performance. The mountaineer, for example, may be admired for his qualities of character and achievements but may yet derive greater pleasure from the *manner* of his doing rather than in what he manages to do. To arrive at the summit is one thing but to arrive there in a novel and technically demanding way is another. The mountaineer can sometimes enter into a kind of psycho-drama acting out his most cherished ideals and standards. Only when these are fulfilled, in the form of courage, coolness, technical accomplishment, strength, stamina and judgment, is he fully satisfied. The true mountaineer is not deluded by arrogance or conceit. There is no demand for public acclaim. If there is talk of conquest it is not of the mountain but of self. It is from the realization of self as a mountaineer that, in one's own estimation, one *becomes* a mountaineer.

Similarly 'the well-played game', from the performer's perspective, is not just one that is evenly fought and fairly conducted, but one that, especially from the aesthetic point of view, is experienced as a kind of sporting *oeuvre* in which all the player's skills and intelligence in the form of 'know-how', are put to the test and not found wanting. What is done is harnessed to a purpose, yet in the doing of what is required there is richness and variety. 'The well-played game' is not only presented as an exemplary case of what *that* game is and what it can offer, (such as in that classic Wimbledon final in 1975 between Arthur Ashe and Jimmy Connors), but is experienced by the players in a way that is comparable to the experience a connoisseur of wine might find in the taste of a good Burgundy, or the experience a violinist might find in the exquisite playing of a Haydn string quartet.

Related to the notion of 'the well-played game' is 'the good contest'. The emphasis here is not in perceiving a game as if it were an artistic *genre* but in terms of struggle and strife. In 'the good strife', writes Metheny, (1965) 'men treat each other as partners in a common enterprise; in "the bad strife" they treat each other as animals or things' (pp.41–2). Implicit in the good contest is the original meaning of the word competition, meaning 'to question and strive together'. The good contest is not as sport can sometimes become, a gladiatorial combat marked by violence and brutishness, but one which is characterized by full-blooded challenge and effort in an atmosphere of uncompromising but friendly rivalry.

For the performer it is not a destructive or humiliating form of experience but an enobling and edifying one. Each contestant is grateful to the other for being an honourable and worthy opponent. Each will emerge from 'the good contest' more fulfilled than when he entered it. Each will have discovered something more about himself that he did not know was there before.

A correlative aspect of 'the good contest', as others have recognized (Kaelin, 1979, p.329; Arnold, 1979a, pp.159–60), is the building up and release of tensions. Arnold (1979c, p.160) suggests that each sport provides its own framework for the control, arousal and easement of tensions. A sport's very rules and procedures, to some extent, determine what is likely to be experienced. In tennis, for example, the punctuation of the game into 'points', 'games' and 'sets' produces a staccato-like build up and release of tension, whereas in a sport like track cycle racing, it is focussed largely on 'the break' for the finish. Each sport, because of its own distinctive structure, offers different experiential possibilities. For many competitors these awakening and excitatory psychosomatic rhythms become a part of a contest's intrinsic enjoyment. In this respect the 'good contest' is not unlike a sexual encounter where a mounting of tension is followed by its pleasurable discharge.

The 'good contest' can be thought of as an uplifting form of sporting experience. It derives from the institutionalization of a human activity but transcends any description of its logically stateable purpose. For the participant the value of the 'good contest' lies not in victory or defeat but in the qualitative process of engagement. This, from the aesthetic point of view, is what is important.

Summary

What has been suggested is firstly that at school level aesthetic education is best conceived as learning how to engage in different forms of activity rather than be concerned only with the critical study of them. Secondly, in so far as aesthetic education relates to movement it can be shown that physical activities can be logically divided into three categories — the non-aesthetic, the partially aesthetic and those which can be considered arts. Thirdly while recognizing this categorization it has, at the same time, been demonstrated that aesthetic perception or experience in movement is not confined to those activities that are designated arts. Fourthly, despite the aesthetic perspective of the performer and spectator sharing large areas of common ground, there, nonetheless, remain some interesting and identifiable differences between them.

Notes

1   For a well argued criticism of Hirst's view see Gingell (1975) and for White's view see Wilson (1980).
2   See Arnold (1979a).
3   Further discussion on the education of feelings and emotions can be found in Best (1985) and Dunlop (1984).
4   Carlisle's argument (1969) is based upon this premise.
5   See Maheu (1962), for example.
6   The notion of embodiment is an interesting one and has a number of different connotations. For one explanation of what embodiment entails see Arnold (1979b), especially pages 1–14.
7   For an elaboration of this point see Wittgenstein (1953, p.23).
8   There is not the time or space here to go into the problematic area of 'empathy' or the sort of involvement the 'fan' experiences. For further reading on both these points see Arnold (1979b, p.154; also pp.71–85 and 110–5).
9   Kaelin (1979, p.329) speaks of creative perception as a movement of the human body. Also Merleau-Ponty (1949) observes that an artist thinks with his material, not with the ideas he imposes on them.
10 Strawson (1967, pp.5–13) makes a similar distinction as the one being made here when he refers to 'participant enjoyments' and 'spectator enjoyments'.

11 A helpful article on the fusion of form and feeling in art see Berndtson (1960).
12 Arnold (1979b) and Bouet (1969) are exceptions in this respect.
13 Quote taken from Lowe (1977, p.257). No precise details given.
14 Salvan (1966, p.66) in writing of the phenomenon of 'togetherness' or the lived experience of *being* with others observes: 'It is intimately felt in the common rhythm of the powers; each one of them feels within himself the same movement of transcendence toward a common goal, on the horizon of a common world, and feels it *with* the other rowers.'

7   Creativity, Self Expression and Dance

In the last chapter reference was made of the aesthetic to art and it was seen that although they have some things in common they are by no means interchangeable. The same is true of the creative and the aesthetic. Although in some educational literature[1] they are frequently juxtaposed as if they were the same this is, of course, not the case. Just as it is possible to aesthetically experience or appreciate something (for example, a natural or art object) and not be creative, so it is possible to be creative (for example, invent a new type of computer or explosive device) without *necessarily* being aesthetic. Although creativity is perhaps most readily associated with the arts, it is by no means confined to them. Creativity can occur in science no less than in mathematics or history[2].

The Meaning of Creativity

The traditional view of creativity is that it is an inexplicable form of 'divine inspiration' which somehow can take mortals by the hand so to speak and mysteriously and miraculously get them to produce works of genius in a variety of forms but especially, it would seem, in the realms of painting music and literature[3]. More recently, however, creativity has come to be a general term of approval for those acts that lead to the solution of problems or the ability, at least, to think in an open, divergent and non-conformist way [4]. Conceptually, however, the meaning of creativity is characterized by reference to at least four conditions. These will be referred to as the *novel* condition; the *relevance* condition; the *conflict* condition; and the *evaluative* condition.

The novelty condition recognizes that creativity is indispensably related to that which is new or different in some way. The great creative achievements of the past, whether by Copernicus, Galileo, Einstein, Shakespeare, Handel or Picasso are marked by originality. Some philosophers would in the case of scientific achievement prefer to use the word 'discovery' since the scientist as a seeker of truth reveals something that is already there, such as the 'laws of relativity', rather than 'creating' something which did not exist previously, such as Stravinsky's *Le Sacre du Printemps*[5]. Even if this distinction is accepted as adequately separating scientific achievements from artistic ones it will be seen that in terms of human culture and understanding the factor of *novelty* remains common to both.

In noting what has been said so far it will have been appreciated that the condition of novelty on its own does not make an act or an idea creative: it must also be *relevant* to a given situation or field of endeavour. Thus Einstein's 'creative' achievements were in terms of physics and Stravinsky's in terms of music. Each was confronted with what might loosely be called a 'problem solving' situation in a particular and recognizable cultural context.

It will be appreciated further, however, that a creative product cannot be new in all respects, especially if it comes from a field of human endeavour which has a long and established tradition. The question of novelty must therefore be seen as a relative one. Unless one believes in creation *ex nihilo* (which in terms of human comprehension makes it unintelligible) it will invariably arise from and come into *conflict* with an activity's rules and conventions. As Olford (1971) expresses the point: 'To say that "X is creative" is to claim that X exceeds proper expectations enshrined in established criteria of excellence or correctness' (p.81). In this sense creativity in a given field can occur in one of two main ways. The first refers to the fact that the creative act may extend, or go beyond, the existing background in some way. Conflict here is perhaps more properly expressed as 'modification', as when, for example, Newtonian physics transformed what had been inherited from the tradition of Galileo and Kepler. The second way of exceeding conventional expectations, and one which is more radical, is to actually alter or replace established criteria, as Einstein did with Newtonian physics, by superseding it with a quite different theory. In such culturally significant achievements creativity is to be seen not so much in terms of modification but rather in terms of 'transcendence'[6]. Put somewhat poetically the greatest of creative achievements come about as a result of the successful thinking of 'forbidden thoughts'. Such achievements revolutionize a mode of endeavour rather than modify it. What it is important to realize, however, is that creativity or the condition of novelty demands a background out of which something new can emerge.

It was suggested that a fourth condition of creativity is that what is produced or achieved must be valued in some way. That is to say it must be positively *evaluated* as meeting certain standards. These will relate to, if not be identical with, the public criteria by which a particular human activity is identified and judged. Thus 'artistic creativity' is appraised according to the cannons of what is considered good or bad in art. The same is true of science and other fields of endeavour. As White (1975) puts it: 'how far we are prepared to call them (i.e. scientists or artists) 'creative' seems to vary according to the value of their discoveries as assessed by the intrinsic standards of their discipline' (p.132). Although this comment of White's overlooks the point concerning transcendence made above, it does reinforce the necessity of having a relevant background in order to make judgments of worth. It is only by and through the criteria that are associated with and imminent in a particular form of activity, which is already valued, that the term creativity is most readily understood. Thus it is usually the case that creative work in any of a culture's valued pursuits is normally regarded as a good thing. It is something to be commended.

The Logical Priority of Product Over Process

In contrast to the product account of creativity given above, creativity is sometimes spoken of as if it were some sort of inner or mental process or series of processes[7] which may or may not result in something tangible. The point about the relationship of process to product, however, is that the former only makes sense in terms of the latter. It is only by reference to something that can be characterized as creative that the phrase 'creative process' can be made intelligible. Hence, it is necessary to be clear about what a creative product is before being able to study its possible psychological correlates.

What is being argued here is that there is a logical priority of the 'product account' of the meaning of creativity over what might be referred to as the 'process account'. To adjudge somebody as being creative is to refer to something that a person has produced and not merely to psychological events he has undergone. It refers not to private processes but to publically evaluated products. To put the matter another way: it is only by reference to a person's distinctive achievements within a particular field of endeavour that creative people come to be recognized for what they are. Great artists and composers of the past are considered creative because of what they 'brought forth' in the form of paintings and music, not because of what may be known about the processes they underwent in producing them. It should be appreciated in making this point that it does not imply or deny that there may be some independently identifiable psychological processes or personality traits associated with creativity. Nor is it being suggested that some attempt should not be made to study these as 'scientific' facts (as, of course, has been the case)[8]. What *is* being denied is that they can exist or be studied as *creative* psychological processes or as 'traits' of creativity unless it is clear what the *concept* of creativity entails. Briskman (1980) neatly summarizes what is being maintained here by saying that:

> although we can describe the creativity of the product without reference to any psychological process, we *cannot* describe the creativity of some psychological process without reference to any products. This is true for two reasons: first, because the process is a creative one *only* if it issues in a product deemed to be a creative one; and secondly, because any process worthy of the name 'creative' will involve an ineliminable interaction with 'intermediary' products which help to create the psychological states of the creator. (p.93)

Both these points have significance for education, not least as they relate to the place of dance within the movement curriculum. Before, however, pursuing this point further with particular reference to 'self-expression', it will be helpful to say something about creativity in relation to education.

Creativity and Education

Creativity has so far been discussed in terms of an individual achieving something of cultural significance. In this absolute sense the creative person is one who makes a unique contribution in art or science or some other valued form of endeavour. Clearly, however, school children cannot be expected to be creative if measured against such exacting standards. In the context of education, therefore, creativity is perhaps best looked upon not in cultural or absolute terms but in biographically relative ones. Creative behaviour in schools more reasonably refers, as Ausubel and Floyd (1969) suggest, to productions which are novel only in relation to 'an individual's past experience' (p.533). In this modified version of creativity it can refer to a child who invents, thinks, makes or produces something which is new to him, even though it may have been replicated many times before by others. The desire for creativity in education stems largely from the child–centred view, which maintains that creativity is a good thing because it helps promote individual freedom and autonomy. It assists in some way, it is thought, the quest for self-actualization and personal identity. Utilitarian thinkers also argue that teaching for creativity should be encouraged because cultural (not to say national) advancement, and all this means for economic efficiency and competition, depends upon it. Regardless, however, of the reasons for the recent upsurge in the idea of promoting creativity as a concern of education there is an expressed belief that 'creativity is not a special gift of the selected few. It is instead a property shared by all humanity, to a greater or smaller degree' (Foster, 1971, p.8). It maintains that 'creativity is within the realm of each individual depending upon the area of expression and capability of the individual' (Fliegler, 1961, p.14).

The belief that every child has creative potential may be a romantic one. Nonetheless, it is not unreasonable to suggest that education should provide some opportunity for its promotion and development and that this should take place within the context of particular curriculum activities. Within the movement curriculum the best hope, it would seem, of fostering creativity is within dance. This is so firstly because it is an aesthetic activity and it is generally recognized that there is more freedom and scope for creativity in an aesthetic activity than a non–aesthetic or sporting one. Secondly, dance, especially when composition is involved, demands that one should be creative in either an absolute or relative sense.

Self Expression and Aesthetic Education

The relationship of self-expression to creativity and the aesthetic is an important one and in order to be clear about what is not meant by self-expression in this context it will be necessary first to distinguish two other forms so that possible confusion is avoided later.

Self-expression in its *naturalistic sense* is perhaps best characterized as a form of emotional discharge which results from an unreflective reaction to a situation or event as when, for example, a child might 'beam with happiness', 'sigh with relief', or 'scream in terror'. The point about naturalistic expression is that it is often symptomatic of a particular state or feeling and free of deliberate teaching or learning.

What occurs is spontaneous and uninhibited. It may or may not be socially acceptable. It is a form, as Dewey (1958) once put it, of 'self-exposure' (p.62). It is, for better or worse, simply a fact of life and an indication of our humanity. Self-expression in this first sense is something every teacher should understand and take account of in his teaching in order to be effective but it is not central to his purpose as an educator.

The second form of self-expression which is sometimes invoked in the name of education and aesthetic activities in particular, is what might be described as *therapeutic*. It is sometimes said, for example, that activities like 'creative writing', singing, music, painting, pottery, carving, drawing, instrumental music, drama and dance, keep the child and/or adolescent, to 'act out' his aggressive tendencies, conflicts and tensions. It is likely that some form of 'catharsis' does take place for many children. Certainly there are many who maintain there is positive connection between the arts and therapy[9]. Be this as it may, the point to be made here is that education is not therapy. The aims and objectives of the teacher are not those of the therapist. Although therapeutic effects may stem from the work of the teacher of aesthetic or expressive activities these are not the reason for his teaching them. As teacher he is concerned with introducing the pupil to these activities for their own inherent values rather than for other benefits which may fortuitously accrue as a result of engaging in them. The purpose of the educator is not that of the therapist, even though the outcome of what occurs may in fact to some extent overlap.

It has been suggested that neither 'naturalistic' or 'therapeutic' self-expression is something with which the teacher is primarily concerned. Self-expression in education, especially perhaps as it relates to creativity and aesthetic subjects, espouses the principle of 'not into the child, but from the child'. This, however, must not be viewed as an unbridled form of 'doing as you please' so much as a carefully monitored balance between freedom and discipline. As Dearden (1968) puts it, in its educational sense, 'self-expression is to be contrasted with imposition from without as involving an exercise of choice in which we reveal our personal tastes, preferences and hence distinctive style of individual response' (p.146). He continues 'its aesthetic value will depend upon the understanding we possess', and makes the point that 'the self-expression of an educated person is an exercise of choice implicitly or explicitly guided by reference to criteria'. It should be noted here that although there can be no aesthetic self-expression without choice, it does not follow that the provision of choice on its own will lead to aesthetic self-expression. Put another way, opportunity for choice is only a necessary, but not a sufficient, condition of aesthetic self-expression.

It has been suggested above that self-expression in its educational sense involves both freedom and discipline and that in what might loosely be called 'creative and aesthetic activities' there is need for this relationship to be more clearly understood. The first point to be made here is that there is need to have a knowledge and understanding of the medium or activity in which one is participating. Another way to put this is to say that there is a good deal to learn about the conventions and rules of a practice before one can reasonably be expected to exercise choice within it. Freedom of choice can only arise from a known background of possibility. Although, as has been shown, creative self-expressive in its absolute sense entails going beyond the rules, the rules must first be known before they can be meaningfully transcended. Writing of creativity in dance, Chapman (1972) observes:

> If, in order to be creative (or aesthetically self-expressive), children or students are to exercise choice, they need to be shown what choices can be made, and they require some criteria which will enable them to discriminate, to make critical judgments.' (p.18)

Related to a background knowledge in the form of the rules and conventions of an activity, is the question of a particular activity's skills and techniques. Clearly without the necessary wherewithal little can be started, let alone achieved. It is because of this it is somewhat empty to speak of freedom without discipline. Hence Best (1982) is right in maintaining that 'if children do not acquire certain techniques, whether of language, the arts, or any other subjects, they are deprived of certain possibilities for freedom of expression and individuality' (p.285). Unless children are taught the particular techniques and skills associated with different aesthetic activities they will not know how to express themselves. What is not always appreciated by some child-centred 'free expressionists', is that freedom for creativity and self-expression are not restricted by technical competency but actually enhanced by it. More than this it is necessary to realize that the teaching of appropriate skills and techniques, far from inhibiting or distorting freedom of creativity and self-expression, is the only clear way of making it possible.

What follows from what has been said so far is that if children are to be creative and/or self-expressive in an aesthetic activity like dance, it is important that they should have acquired some knowledge of the medium in the form of critical understanding and some skill in the form of a 'movement vocabulary'. What else, however, is demanded? I would suggest some use of their imaginative powers in the sense of putting what they know and can do into new and fresh forms of their own choosing. It is in play that the child is most naturally and imaginatively expressive. In pretending to be a coalman or acting out the role of a nurse he reveals something of his perception of what these people do. The child draws upon what is known and makes up what he does not. What results is often a mixture of reality and fantasy. He is both imitative and imaginary. He both follows the rules and departs from them. According to Warnock (1977) imagination is 'the power to see possibilities, beyond the immediate; to perceive and feel the boundlessness of what is before one, the intricacies of a problem, the complications or subtleties of something previously scarcely noticed' (p.155). What imagination in dance (as well as in other aesthetic subjects) demands is the ability to see the possibility for the expression of ideas, moods, emotions and so on *in an aesthetic way*. It involves taking account of established criteria and well tried techniques in order to explore and present something which can be both appreciated and appraised.

Opportunity for self-expression in dance comes both through 'interpretation' as well as through 'creative composition'. In the former use it is not so much *what* is to be expressed but rather *how* best to go about it. The plot of *West Side Story* or an episode from *Fame*, for example, may be decided upon but the manner in which it is thought through and presented may be left entirely open. It should be noted that it is possible to be both imaginative and expressive without necessarily being creative, either in an absolute or relative sense. In 'creative composition', however, there is the demand not only for imaginative interpretation but the inception and hatching of something new which has not been thought of or attempted before. Creative composition refers to the *making* of dances rather than to the *learning* and/or interpreting of them. It requires not only originality but a clear grasp of aesthetic criteria and technical know-how so that what is conceived can be successfully born.

It is sometimes said that the teacher's most important role in getting children to be creative and expressive is the establishment of an encouraging, stimulating yet secure atmosphere[10]. The climate, of course, of any educational situation is important, and it may be that this is particularly true for 'aesthetic subjects'. In recognizing this, however, it should never be forgotten that a teacher's prime function is to initiate pupils into activities with understanding and technical competency so that they have the means by and through which self-expression can take place. Without understanding and without technical competency aesthetic self-expression in any educated sense will be rendered impossible.

Dance and Aesthetic Education

In speaking of the possibilities of dance as a creative and self-expressive aesthetic activity little has so far been said directly about the criteria to which reference can and should be made when dance is being either taught or appraised. What follows is but a brief introduction to each of these topics in the light of what has been previously discussed.

In teaching dance, as an art form, such *formal properties* as 'rhythm', 'symmetry' and 'harmony' or *compositional* ones in terms of 'balance', 'continuity', 'proportion', 'unity', 'repetition' and 'contrast', are of key importance, as are such *expressive qualities* as 'strength', 'dynamism', 'boldness' and 'weakness' or 'pity', 'fear', 'anger' and 'sadness'. The pedagogic point to be made here is that such concepts should not be learnt in a detached or independent way apart from the dance as if somehow this was a prior logical necessity, but rather as part and parcel of its enlightened practice. To be an educated dancer entails in considerable degree aesthetic understanding. It means being able to embody what one aesthetically comprehends in terms of the dance. In the artistic performance aesthetic understanding is (or should be) presented in an aesthetically meaningful way. An aesthetic education in terms of the dance involves the giving, or an attempt at giving, an artistic presentation of what is aesthetically understood. In teaching dance one will or should be inescapably concerned with an introduction to aesthetic concepts and aesthetic criteria. These will or should develop and grow out of the inherent demands of dance rather than be separately learnt and artificially applied. This is not to say that the independent study of aesthetic terminology should not be encouraged. Clearly on occasions this can prove valuable. What is being emphasized here is that in schools priority should be given to getting pupils to engage in artistic pursuits which, if well taught, will entail aesthetic understanding rather than merely study in a somewhat critically detached and uninvolved way, aesthetic terminology and works of art, valuable though this may occasionally be.

When a dance is aesthetically evaluated, like any other work of art, it impels reference to objective criteria by means of which it can be judged. This is not a matter of applying predetermined criteria as if the merit of a work can somehow be checked out by (means) of ticks and crosses but of imaginatively entering into a relationship with it. In order to aesthetically appraise something it is first necessary to see it in terms of its own inherent qualities and not in terms of some instrumental or extrinsic purpose. Although there are objective pointers so to speak, it would be a mistake to think that there is a set of characteristics which guaranteed that any created artifice manifesting these characteristics would, necessarily make it meritorious. Kant's doctrine of the 'singularity' of aesthetic judgment indeed denies that there are any general rules for making or judging works of art. A performance in dance simply cannot, as some people might wish, be appraised in accordance with a set of rules which are formulated in advance and which are used as a sort of judgmental rod.

What instead is required in aesthetically appraising something is a personal and imaginative response which may or may not call upon established criteria. To say of a dance that it has 'unity', 'intensity' and 'complexity'; that it is integrated and 'coherently structured'; that it displays a 'wide range of subtle movements'; that it is 'original', 'authentic', 'powerful' and 'emotionally moving', is likely to be saying of it that it is considered praiseworthy. It is to say of *that* dance that it is good because it convincingly presents and is characterized by those aesthetic qualities which can be pointed to and to an extent spoken about. To appraise dance as an art form is to look at it from an aesthetic point of view and to evaluate it in terms of aesthetic criteria that are *relevant* to it. Although aesthetic criteria are *publically* available they are always *particularly* applied. It is a myth to think of artistic appraisal in terms of general criteria which are universally applicable to all works of art. It is precisely because works of art are distinctive that they require distinctive appraisals be made of them.

The teacher of dance, knowing all this, will not expect from her pupils when they are asked to appraise what they or their classmates have done, a ritualistic and automatic reference to established criteria but an informed, critical and sensitive response to what has been presented. What the good teacher of dance will look for is not a well rehearsed formula-like appeal to aesthetic qualities but a genuine judgment based upon an intelligent but aesthetically perceptive and individual viewpoint.[11]

Notes

1 See, for example, the Munn Report (1977).
2 Some writers on creativity, on the other hand, do reserve the term for

original work done on the arts, maintaining that whereas artists 'create', scientists 'discover' truths, and historians 'uncover' facts from the past.

3   The book edited by Brewster Ghiselin (1952) called *The Creative Process* reveals something of the idiosyncratic nature of how creative persons go about their work.

   PE Veron's edited collection (1972) on *Creativity* is also of interest.

4   For a useful summary of such approaches, especially as they relate to education, see Ausubel and Floyd (1969), particularly pages 532–45.

5   RK Elliott (1971, p.143) wants to preserve the distinction between scientific discovery as an achievement of knowledge and artistic creativity in the form of bringing something 'into being' which can be 'contemplated and admired'.

6   This term, in contrast to the idea of modification, has been taken from Briskman (1980, p.96).

7   A nomenclature which is sometimes adopted in speaking of the creative process is that of Wallas (1926) in which he identified four recognizable phases: preparation, incubation, illumination and verification.

8   A useful summary of creativity in relation to the person is provided by Kneller (1967, pp.62–76).

9   See, for example, the compilation of writings by Waller and Gilroy (1978).

10 This point is again emphasized in a recent publication by the Scottish Committee on Expressive Arts in the Primary School (p.3).

11 For a helpful book about aesthetics in relation to dance see Redfern (1983). See also Redfern (1984).

8 Education, Schooling and the Concept of Movement

In the light of some distinctions that it will be necessary to make in connection with the place of movement in the curriculum it will be helpful if some preliminary observations are made concerning the relationship between education and what in recent years has become known as 'schooling'[1]. It should be noted that in its broadest sense schooling refers to everything that goes on in a school, including education. The narrower and more specific sense in which I propose to use the term, however, in order to differentiate it from what is often called a liberal education, refers to those other necessary or desirable aspects of school life which are pursued for extrinsic reasons rather that intrinsic ones. It will be seen, therefore, that 'schooling' in this second or more restricted sense is not synonymous with education nor confined to it. Whereas education implies the transmission of something worthwhile for its own sake, schooling implies pursuing an activity as a means to something else.

Today the basic sense of 'school' is that it is a special institution created and maintained by society in order to transmit aspects of its culture by means of purposeful teaching and learning to the next generation. The case for schooling rests on the broad argument that there are certain things we want children to acquire, or be provided with, which cannot be as well provided for at home or by the general social environment. As a result the school today, despite recent attempts by some radical thinkers[2], remains something of a place apart from the mainstream of life and is staffed by those who are knowledgeable or expert in some way. The real question for the *educationist* about the role of the school in society, revolves around the question: Which values are of most worth? Difficult and controversial as this question is, education can be seen as an attempt to awaken in the young a capacity to recognize the good and the worthwhile. It carries with it the implicit prescription that once the good and the worth-while have been identified they *ought* to be pursued. Clearly what constitutes the good and worthwhile is an old and controversial matter[3]. Insofar as it relates to education, however, the answer that has been provided in this book is that it is an initiation of pupils into those valued pursuits of an 'academic' and 'physical' kind for their own sake and in a morally defensible manner. What this involves with regard to the latter has been the subject of the past few chapters. Briefly put it lies predominantly in the rationality of practical knowledge especially as this is (or should be) exemplified by an engagement in particular activities. This not only recognizes the educative value of 'knowing how' to perform with competency and understanding in a variety of whole-bodied cultural pursuits but to appreciate, particularly when it is logically necessary to do so, the moral and aesthetic dimensions of what one is doing.

It will be understood, however, that apart from education the school is also concerned with the fulfilment of other necessary or desirable purposes. It is to these other necessary or desirable purposes that the term 'schooling' is ascribed. Schooling then is to be seen in the present context as a general term applying to those valuable or useful aspects of the curriculum that do not necessarily meet the criterial demands of education. In particular it highlights the difference between pursuing an activity for its own instrinsic worth and pursuing it for the sake of something else. Whereas education is associated with doing certain activities for the values immanent in them, schooling is associated more with doing things for instrumental reasons or purposes that lie outside them. Barrow (1981) recognizes that there is a place for both 'education' and 'schooling' in the curriculum when he writes:

> in bringing up our children, besides educating them and socializing them, we should have an eye on their future employment; besides giving them an education for its own sake, we should try to develop their talents and then match them to likely opportunities, for the sake of their livelihood and satisfaction and society's smooth functioning'. (p.59)

What becomes apparent is that the school as a social institution should not only be concerned with education in the sense that it can liberate, as Bailey (1984) puts it, from the 'present and particular' (p.29) by an involvement of pupils in intrinsically worthwhile ends but that it should also be concerned with, and take some responsibility for, other necessary or desirable purposes such as a preparation for work or the promotion of health. There need be no confusion or conflict between them providing the distinctions made remain clear. Regrettably this is not always done so that when it comes to writing syllabuses for the curriculum the aims and objectives of each often overlap and cause difficulty and confusion as to what is being attempted and how each can be taught and assessed. This is not only apparent in a number of textbooks on 'physical education' but also in many 'physical education' syllabuses that have been developed recently for examination purposes. The key differentiating question for the teacher is: 'Are the activities being taught considered in themselves as worthwhile ends (education) or are they seen primarily as a means to further an extrinsic purpose (schooling)?'

It was intimated above that a central instance of schooling is 'vocational training'. Here the prime concern is not to initiate pupils into a love of an activity for its own sake but rather to equip them to become more readily employable. The point of this branch of schooling is to provide pupils with a specific set of skills so that they can subsequently be capable of doing a particular job in order to earn their living whether as typist, bricklayer or plumber. The several different schemes encouraged and sponsored by the Manpower Services Commission are precisely of this type.

Whatever reservations one may have about the quality and viability of some of them the point is that they have become a part of the curriculum because from the utilitarian point of view they are considered as serving a necessary purpose.

Another instance of the schooling curriculum, often associated with individual and social welfare, is that of 'physical fitness and health'[4]. This is often stated as an objective of 'physical education'. It will be appreciated, however, that if 'physical education' is to be understood in terms of the intrinsic worth of physical activities it cannot, without confusion, refer also to a purpose that lies beyond them. One of the problems in the use of the term 'physical education' is that it does this not only in connection with 'health and fitness' but with other such extrinsic, if desirable purposes, such as, for example, a 'preparation for the wholesome use of leisure'. It is because of this unsatisfactory ambivalence in the term 'physical education', as it is commonly used, that it is best forsaken and replaced by the term movement. The great advantage of the term movement is that it allows reference to be made to both education and schooling without confusing the one with the other.

Perhaps enough has been said to make the point that the place of physical activities in the curriculum can be justified both in terms of 'education' and 'schooling'. The difference between them lies not so much in *what* is taught but in *how* and *why* they are taught?[5]

The Concept of Movement

The concept of movement, it has been suggested, provides opportunity for the curriculum planner to reconcile the demands of education with those of schooling. To recognize this is not to weaken the position of movement in the curriculum but is rather to strengthen it for it is no longer solely dependent upon an educational justification for its inclusion.

How then is movement best explicated as a 'subject' in the context of the school and its curriculum? I propose to attempt to answer to this question by looking at what I shall call the three dimensions of movement. These are :

> Dimension I   — 'About' Movement
> Dimension II — 'Through' Movement
> Dimension III — 'In' Movement

It should be stressed that these three dimensions of movement are not mutually exclusive. On the contrary they overlap and interrelate with one another. They are only separated here for the purpose of analysis and clarification. In the school situation this should not only be realized but actively brought about by a structured programme of work.

Dimension I — 'About' Movement

Education 'about' movement can be looked upon as a rational form of enquiry, concerned with the answering of such questions as: How is the body organized to support and control movement? What effect does movement have on the living organism? How is growth related to motor control? How does man best learn to move in different ways? In what ways does movement, or lack of it, influence the development of the personality? What part does movement play in facilitating interaction and communication? What place does movement have in the cultural study of man? What are the best ways of classifying, analyzing and notating movement?

As a subject of study movement is concerned with human motion in all its richness and diversity. In the school situation, however, it will be concerned particularly with that family of physical activities which comprises sports and games, athletics, swimming, gymnastics, modern and ethnic dance, and outdoor pursuits such as rock climbing, canoeing and orienteering. By calling upon such areas as anatomy, physiology, physics, psychology, sociology, anthropology, aesthetics and philosophy it can be regarded as comprising a composite area of study and investigation. At the primary or elementary school level the theme of 'movement' might be taken as a project with reference to people's pastimes and games much in the same way that a project on the 'planets', 'seas' and 'rivers' or 'fuels' might be. Also such movement ideas as running, jumping, throwing and catching; or turning, twisting, curling and stretching might be introduced, observed and practised. In the upper reaches of the secondary school, however, by which time a good deal of general background knowledge will have been assimilated, there is no reason why a knowledge about movement should not become a good deal more discrete and broken down into such specialized areas of study as human growth and development; the physiology of exercise; the biomechanics of particular activities, motor learning and skill acquisition, the place and function of dance in different cultures, the evolution of games in nineteenth century England, sport and leisure in contemporary society. It will be seen that such component areas as these lend themselves to various forms of assessment if this is desired.

Movement as a 'field of study' is a composite 'discipline' and as such is concerned with the understanding of a 'portion of reality — that is its description, its explanation and sometimes its prediction' (Kengon, 1968, p.164). Insofar as movement in this academic or theoretical sense is 'professionally orientated towards education it must necessarily be selective in its content and attentive to changing people in some way for the better in a coherent course of study which highlights what can be said about movement in a rational way and be capable of providing satisfactory answers to such questions as: What is its aim? What activities are to be taught? What methods are to be employed? How is the curriculum programme to be assessed?

It will be appreciated then that education 'about' movement is predominantly concerned with the transmission of propositional knowledge and is capable of being presented in a discursive way. It is public and objective, in principle shareable, and therefore communicable. It has the merit of providing a theoretical background of understanding which helps make coherent and meaningful that which is observed and performed. In this respect knowing 'about' movement can act as an analytical, critical and evaluative aspect of movement education.

Dimension II — 'Through' Movement

The idea of learning 'through' movement is still perhaps most commonly associated with the term 'physical education' but, as has been shown, if the difference between 'education' and 'schooling' is not to be lost the term 'physical education' is best avoided for it confusingly conflates the intrinsic values of physical activities with those which are extrinsic. In the literature, physical education is not only ambiguous in terms of its objectives but carries with it an implicit dualism which suggests a separation of mind from body.

In the context of the school curriculum the 'through' dimension of movement is best conceived of as being instrumental in purpose. It can then be looked upon as being able to assist (a) in the promotion of educational objectives which are not its own; or (b) in the promotion of other necessary or desirable objectives of a 'non-educational' kind. The dimension of 'through' movement is therefore an adaptable and flexible one. Even within academically orientated areas of the curriculum it can be profitably employed. Here it will entail the intelligent utilization of those situations that arise, or can intentionally be made to arise, in the teaching of physical activities that can assist in the initiation of pupils into what are sometimes spoken of as the basic forms of awareness. Thus education 'through' movement can be made to relate to the 'academic' aspect of education in at least two main ways:

(i) it can be 'illustrative' of something that has arisen in another context; or,

(ii) it can throw up problems and issues of its own which are unlikely to be resolved unless they are 'referred back' to one or more of the basic forms of knowledge.

For the sake of convenience I will call respectively these two main ways of relating movement to education in its academic sense as the 'illustrative function' and the 'referrent function'.

The illustrative function

The illustrative function is perhaps best understood in terms of the question 'How can I, the teacher, get children to better understand what they have learnt in the classroom through the active use of their bodies or through the concomitant activities that form a part of movement?'

It may be, for example, that mechanical principles arising in science can be put to the test and made more meaningful by the pupils using themselves or their fellows as subjects. In such activities as athletics, diving, trampolining and gymnastics, theory can be transformed into practice. The track, pool and gymnasium can become an extension of the laboratory. Apart from the possibility of transforming something inert and abstract into something fresh and meaningful, the active use of one's own body in learning can have several other effects which can assist the growth of knowledge and understanding. It can help 'personalize' knowledge[6]: it can give a new perspective on the same material; it can help illuminate and give a greater insight into what in a sense is already 'known'; and it can act as a secondary reinforcing process.

The referent function

The referent function, like the illustrative function, is best understood in terms of a question. Let us take the activity of dance. It may be that at some stage in a lesson the question will arise 'What is it that makes dance dance?' It is not long before a host of other questions are raised to do with such notions as expression, rhythm, line, form, illusion and so on. It is inevitable if such questions persist that one is led back into that branch of knowledge called aesthetics.

A second example of the referent function can arise in the case of games. In this situation it may happen that a question like 'Why is it necessary to have rules?' will be asked. If the educationist is to take the query seriously it may lead on to a consideration of the purpose of rules, their function and their justification or otherwise. Such concepts as freedom, equality and justice, as has been shown, are related to such notions as 'sportsmanship' and 'fair play' and are as applicable on the field of play no less than off it.

Similarly, when activities are expressly taught with a view to promoting the concerns of schooling they can be justified as being worthy of inclusion in the curriculum if it can be shown that they are the best or at least a good means in the promotion of other purposes that are considered useful or desirable in some way. Thus, if it can be empirically demonstrated that playing soccer, for example, increases 'socialization' in a number of specific ways then it might reasonably be claimed that soccer is a useful means of improving it. From the point of view of schooling, then, soccer might be taught and justified on the grounds of 'socialization' if it was thought that pupils' needed socializing for various reasons, i.e., they lacked social experience or were anti-social.

The important question for the instrumentalist is not to ask whether physical activities are taught for their own intrinsic values, in an educative way, but whether as a result of them being taught they can be used to serve a necessary or desirable purpose. If in other words movement activities can be shown to be a good means of furthering purposes of a 'non-educative' but nonetheless justifiable kind then there is good reason for including them in the curriculum apart from whatever intrinsic values they may have of their own.

Overall then it will be seen that a case for the *instrumental* use of movement activities in the curriculum can be made as a means of:

(a) promoting educational objectives *other* than those of movement;
or
(b) promoting the objectives of *schooling*.

Examples of the former (a) are:

(i)   scientific understanding;
(ii)   aesthetic understanding and appreciation;
(iii) moral understanding and conduct.

Examples of the latter (b) are:

(i)   social interaction and socialization;
(ii)   fitness and health;
(iii) the wholesome use of leisure time.

It will be appreciated that the degree to which physical activities can be instrumentally used to effect the objectives of 'education' and 'schooling' will always, to one extent or another, be dependent upon the intention, knowledge, imagination and skill of the teacher. What matters especially is that the teacher is able to recognize the difference between the two 'undertakings' and be in a position if necessary to justify each.

All in all the dimension of 'through' movement is best conceived as being that part of the curriculum which can be used as a means of enhancing and harmonizing the physical, intellectual, social and emotional aspects of a growing individual chiefly through professionally selected and directed physical activities.

Dimension III — 'In' Movement

'About' movement has been characterized as being to do with movement as a field or theoretical body of knowledge that can be academically studied in a disinterested way, whereas 'through' movement, it has been said, is to do with the justifiable utilization of that whole-bodied and culturally-based family of physical activities which, with intelligent teaching, can be made to serve values which are not necessarily intrinsic to them. In this third dimension of 'in' movement the concern is with the values that are an inherent part of the activities themselves. To put the matter another way: 'in' movement upholds the view that movement activities, especially when looked at from the 'inside' or participatory perspective of the moving agent[7], are in and of themselves worthwhile. What makes them educational is that:

(i)   they are concerned with a valued aspect of our cultural heritage;

(ii) they exemplify knowledge and understanding of a practical rather than a theoretical kind.

An educational situation or process arises from them in particular when:

(iii) they are entered into and pursued for their own sake and not because of the external or extrinsic benefits they might intentionally, or unintentionally bring;

(iv) they are taught in a morally acceptable manner.

An education 'in' movement like the good life will be a 'mixed' life. It will comprise a number of inherently worthwhile physical activities which are not only recognized to be of value in an 'objective' sense but found to be so in a 'subjective' sense. They are both considered by others valuable and found by the participant to be so. To be in an educative situation with regard to them is not just a question of pursuing them in a perfunctory or prudential way, but of engaging in them because they are found to be meaningful and satisfying enterprises.

It should be made clear that although education in relation to the concept of movement is partially explicated by reference to the dimensions of 'about' and 'through' movement, neither is centrally concerned with movement as a family of meaning laden activities and processes which are of interest in themselves and worth engaging in for the values they inherently contain and sources of satisfaction they offer. It is not that either of the dimensions of 'about' or 'through' are irrelevant to or out of keeping with the notion of 'in' movement. On the contrary, both inevitably feed into it and in their different ways help illuminate it. The three dimensions of the concept of movement then are not separate but functionally related. Each dimension is not exclusive of the others but overlaps and dovetails into them. The concept of movement is a mutually reinforcing and interdependent one. Like a triangle, it has different points of emphasis which come into prominence at different times. If movement were conceived of only in intellectualistic terms or what can be propositionally stated about it, it would be but a hived-off and disembodied academic pursuit. Similarly, if movement were seen only as a means of serving ends other than its own it would remain purely instrumental in character and not worthy of being educative in its own right. For the curriculum implications of the concept of movement to be grasped in an adequate way it must be seen not only as a field of study, and as having an instrumental value, but as a worthwhile group of physical activities to be engaged in for their own inherent worth.

It will be seen that although 'in' movement is largely to do with 'knowing how' to engage in physical activities and in having a direct and lived-body acquaintance of them, the mover who is the author of his movement actions can enrich and bring greater understanding to what he does by a knowledge of 'what is the case', just as he can help realize them by an informed appreciation of appropriate means. There is thus no artificial and watertight divide between the dimensions. The notion of 'in' movement without the employment of some rational knowledge would be intellectually vacuous just as without some utilization of movement as means it would fail to reach certain of its objectives.

The notion of education 'in' movement then is not a self-contained or hived-off entity. Although it emphasizes the agency of the person as mover, it relates to, and draws upon, the other dimensions at different times and in varying degrees according to the situation in hand. To acknowledge this, however, is in no way to detract from movement as a family of whole-bodied activities in which the person can meaningfully engage for no other reason than that he finds them worthy of pursuit. They are, for everyone, potentially in and of themselves interesting and satisfying. They permit the person to actualize the physical dimensions of his being in the form of developed capacities, skilled accomplishments and objective achievements that are in themselves worthwhile. They provide embodied exemplifications of a culture's sporting and dancing heritage that no other subject in the curriculum attempts. Movement in the meeting of its own internal rules, standards and traditions is in and of itself educative. An initiation into the paradigm instances of movement whether sport, dance or outdoor activities, is inherently valuable and therefore should form a part of any school curriculum. What gives them their importance and distinctiveness is that they are culturally significant and physically orientated activities which are concerned with rationality of a practical rather than of a theoretical kind and which are capable of providing those who engage in them with a variety of intrinsic satisfactions as well as a number of extrinsic and unsought after benefits.

Movement and Its Place in the Curriculum

To summarize the arguments that can be made for the inclusion of movement as a 'subject' in the curriculum, apart from practical and administrative ones, are the following. First, recent advances in the articulation of movement as a 'field of study'[8] are now sufficiently well established for it to be regarded as an area of academic interest and worthy of study in its own right. Second, it is possible to justify movement on instrumental grounds if it can be shown that other educative or desirable ends are being served. Third, movement activities, especially perhaps those called sport and dance, are a valued and constituent part of our culture and as such should be transmitted with care from this generation to the next one. Fourth, movement, apart from the provision of distinctive types of whole-bodied, physically demanding, skill-laden and action-based contextual meanings, is the only area of the curriculum which is directly concerned with those experiences of moving which form an integral part of what it is to be a person.

Notes

1   For an introduction to this term see Barrow (1981, p.32–75).
2   Reference here is to such current thinkers as Goodman (1971), Illich (1973) and Reimer (1971), who are at the centre of what has become known as the 'de-schooling' movement. This movement emphasizes two ideas: first, that education and schooling are not necessarily the same thing i.e, the ritual and content should not be confused; second, that the institution of schooling by virtue of it being an institutionalized process causes damage to genuine learning.
3   A useful book which summarizes a number of educational philosophies with reference to their value source is that by Bigge (1982).

Another useful book which summarizes the different value positions of the curriculum process in 'physical education' is that by Jewett and Bain (1985).

4 Many books on physical education state health or fitness or both as objectives of physical education programmes. At primary level, for example, Kirchner (1985, p.9), lists fitness as being one of seven objectives. At secondary level Corbin and Lindsey (1983) place great emphasis on fitness in its various forms, as a part of the 'physical education' programme.

5 An inability to differentiate between education and schooling, between intrinsic and extrinsic values, can lead to the difficulties about aims and objectives. This is not only revealed by Kane's (1976) study referred to in chapter 1, but continues to be a source of difficulty in schools (and colleges) today. In a recent analysis of a sub-committee of the Schools Council (1982, p.49), for example, it is acknowledged that there is a 'lack of agreement about aims and objectives'. This, I suggest, in part stems from the very point I am making.

6 Polanyi (1973) argues that knowledge is never impersonal or completely detached. It always involves some personal participation.

7 For an elaboration of what is entailed here see my book *Meaning in Movement, Sport and Physical Education* (1979b).

8 For a useful summary of the range of disciplines and topics embraced by this phrase consult Brooks (1981). See also such introductory general textbooks as Barrow (1983), Bucher (1983), Larson (1976), Nixon and Jewett (1980), Rivenes (1978), and Gensemer (1985).

9 Rational Planning by Objectives of the Movement Curriculum

In the last chapter the three dimensions of the concept of movement were explicated. It was found that there are both intrinsic and extrinsic reasons for engaging in physical activities as a part of the curriculum and that these respectively are best understood in terms of education and schooling. The distinction between doing something for its own sake because it is intrinsically worthwhile and doing something because it is, or is thought to be, useful in the promotion of something else is an important one and should be clearly borne in mind by all practising teachers. Significant though the 'schooling' aspects of the movement curriculum are, especially perhaps as they relate to such matters as fitness and health and the wholesome use of leisure time, attention in this chapter will be confined to the movement curriculum in its educational or non-utilitarian aspects. This, of course, is in no way to discredit or denigrate the 'schooling' side of the curriculum. Rather it should be seen as an attempt to spell out more clearly than usual what, from the educational point of view, the movement curriculum entails. This is important if the two parts of the movement curriculum are not to be confused one with the other. When it comes to the setting of objectives the recognition of this distinction is crucial.

Basic Factors in Rational Curriculum Planning

If the 'educational' element of the movement curriculum is to proceed in a rational way its values or aims must relate to what is done in terms of the content or selected activities and their objectives as well as to the methods or procedures undertaken. To these three factors some would add a fourth evaluation, so that some sort of assessment and appraisal is made of how effective a programme has been and how it can be altered if necessary to make it more successful. When this four-factor model of curriculum planning is adopted it is now usually acknowledged that the relationship between the factors should be 'cyclical' rather than 'linear' if the teacher/learner process is to be continuous rather than terminal (see figure 1 below).

What should be made clear is that rational curriculum planning (RCP) in the way I intend using the term should not be taken to mean, as it is with some theorists, 'the pre-specification of behavioural outcomes'.[1] Rather it should be understood as being to do with the giving of good reasons for what is decided upon. It involves showing what the grounds are for the adoption of one programme rather than another by an appeal to appropriate evidence, the employment of coherent arguments and the clear expression of a view about the value of physical activities in the general curriculum given the special circumstances of a particular school.

It will be seen that in this endeavour the role of the teacher is of key importance for it is the teacher who is in the best position not only to plan a programme of work but to implement and evaluate it. The general point here is that any action including action about the curriculum takes place within a specific context and a set of traditions.[2]

Figure 1: Basic Factors in Cyclical Rational Curriculum Planning

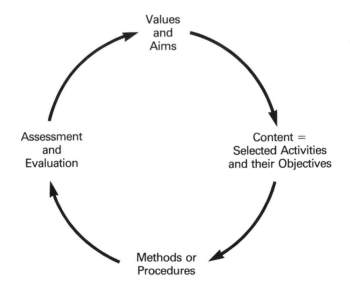

But what is the curriculum? How is it to be conceived and explicated? The word clearly has many connotations of meaning. Some theorists wish it to be confined to those activities which are concerned with education[3] rather than schooling. Other theorists wish to include those elements which are 'hidden' as well as those which are overt and officially timetabled in some way. In order to be clear I propose to use the term to refer to all those planned activities of a school, whether done formally or informally, and which are encouraged and pursued with the interests and welfare of the pupils in mind.

It will include education as well as those elements of schooling which are considered both necessary and desirable. This broader approach to the curriculum is defined by Kerr (1969) as 'all learning which is planned and guided by the school, whether it is carried out in groups or individually, inside or outside the school' (p.16). Such a definition provides a more comprehensive basis for curriculum planning and development.

Underlying Considerations of Rational Curriculum Planning

Lawton (1973) suggests that in planning a curriculum rationally it is necessary to take account of at least three kinds of consideration. Firstly, there are those considerations which derive from *the nature of knowledge* itself. Here it is as well to recall that movement is not only concerned with 'theoretical knowledge' or a knowledge of what is the case and which can be stated propositionally, but also with 'practical knowledge' or a knowledge of how to do or proceed with different forms of activity.[4] Apart from movement being concerned with 'knowing that' and 'knowing how' it is possible, at a less objective level, to speak of 'knowing by acquaintance' which is to do with the performer's kinaesthetic perception of an action, for example, a discus throw. This can arise from the practise of a mastered skill.[5] I shall not here, however, be concerned with this third type of knowledge. Secondly, Lawton suggests, it is necessary to take account of the *nature of the child* or the individual children for whom the curriculum is being planned. The point here, as 'child-centred' educationists emphasize, is that no effective teaching can take place if only the logic of the subject matter is considered instead of also taking into account what is known about 'physical', 'emotional' and 'cognitive' growth and child development in general. As Dewey (1958, p.138) once remarked, it is necessary to 'psychologize' the curriculum in order to facilitate the learning of the pupil. Thirdly, Lawton claims that account must be taken of the *social situation*. Associated with this, and partially stimulated by the Great Debate in the middle and late seventies, is the demand for 'relevance' and 'accountability' in education. Particularly since then movement, like other subjects in the curriculum, has had to provide justificatory arguments for its continued presence as a core subject.[6] It has so far managed to do this, partially on 'cultural heritage', 'practical knowledge' and 'creative and aesthetic' grounds and partially on grounds of health and fitness, socialization and as a preparation for the wholesome use of leisure time in an age when more and more people, young, middle-aged and old, are for various reasons not at work.

Perhaps enough has been said to indicate that rational curriculum planning in movement, as in other subjects, should take account not only of the logic of a carefully selected number of activities, but also of *when* and *how* these activitites are best taught, as well as the intrinsic and extrinsic reasons for doing so. One merit of Lawton's set of considerations is that they ensure that curriculum planning does not go on in a scholastic vacuum. What seems clear is that in the future curriculum planning in schools will not only be made by reference to educational arguments but to other forms of argument such as those to do with vocational training and personal and social welfare. All this is becoming increasingly clear as economic and political pressures are exerted upon schools and what is to be taught in them.[7]

A model of rational curriculum planning which takes account of the above considerations but which in addition attempts to show the relationship between them is shown on next page (see figure 2).

It should be noted that at the centre of this model is the teacher. Ultimately whether or not a curriculum is effective is dependent upon the decisions the teacher makes and the quality of teaching provided. Even allowing for the fact that there is an increased government commitment in a country like Britain to secure greater clarity about the objectives and content of the curriculum by advocating and approving 'national criteria' for different subject areas, the teacher remains at the heart of what it is possible to accomplish. It is the teacher, more than ever perhaps, who will need to take account of his or her professional preparation and see how the factors outlined above apply to his or her particular set of circumstances.

Educational Objectives of the Movement Curriculum

In the last chapter, it was suggested that the concept of movement has three interlocking dimensions — 'about,' 'through' and 'in'. The

Figure 2: Underlying Considerations of Rational Curriculum Planning

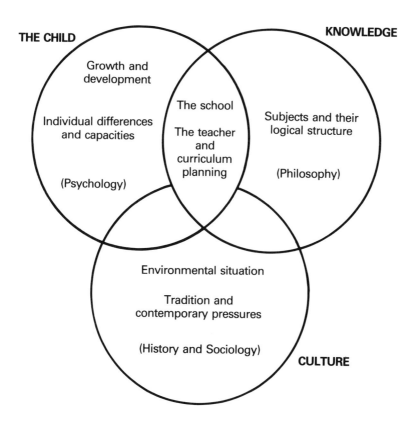

dimension of 'about' movement is concerned with the rational study of movement; the dimension of 'through' movement is concerned with using movement as a vehicle or means of achieving purposes other than its own; and the dimension of 'in' movement is concerned largely with 'knowing how' to participate in different forms of physical activity. Here I shall confine my comments to the first and third of these dimensions as each of them can be justified for inclusion in an educational programme on intrinsic rather than extrinsic grounds. That is to say in the case of the 'about' dimension, a knowledge and understanding of movement is seen in itself to be worthwhile. Similarly, in the case of the 'in' dimension, it is the practice and engagement in physical activities for their own sake that is considered educationally worthwhile and not whether they can be made to serve other purposes such as health, socialization or a preparation for the use of leisure. In an educational context such concerns, if they are gratuitously realized, are best looked upon as 'beneficial outcomes' rather than as 'educational objectives'. The point here is that the spin-off benefits that emerge from the doing of something should not be confused with those values that are inherent in what is done. One of the differences between pursuing an activity for an educational reason, as opposed to a utilitarian one, as has been shown, is that the former sees the activity as valuable in itself whereas the latter sees it only as an instrument or means to bring about something else.[8] In this book I am concerned only with 'educational' objectives. In what follows, therefore, concern will be only with those objectives of the movement curriculum which arise logically from the study and practice of movement for its own sake, regardless of what other utilitarian benefits it may fortuitously also bring.

The dimension of 'about' movement in the curriculum is concerned with three separate but related sets of objectives — the conceptual, the empirical and the informational. They do not necessarily involve an engagement 'in' physical activities and are therefore perhaps best referred to as 'non-participatory objectives'. Further, when it comes to the dimension of 'in' movement I want to suggest that there are again three separate but related sets of objectives for the movement curriculum. These are: prerequisite skill, contextual and expressive. Because the dimension of 'in' movement is *necessarily* concerned with the practice of physical activities I shall refer to them as 'participatory objectives' (see figure 3 on next page).

Together these two groupings of objectives, arising from the concept of movement, constitute and help exemplify the nature of education in the movement curriculum. I shall therefore look at each in turn.

Non-Participatory Objectives

Conceptual objectives

In an important sense it will be appreciated that unless the nature and purpose of an activity is understood it would be difficult to engage in it meaningfully. Certainly to participate successfully in an activity presupposes a knowledge of the rules which characterize it. Without a clear grasp of the rules and conventions of an activity it would make little sense to claim that one knows the activity at all. It will be seen,

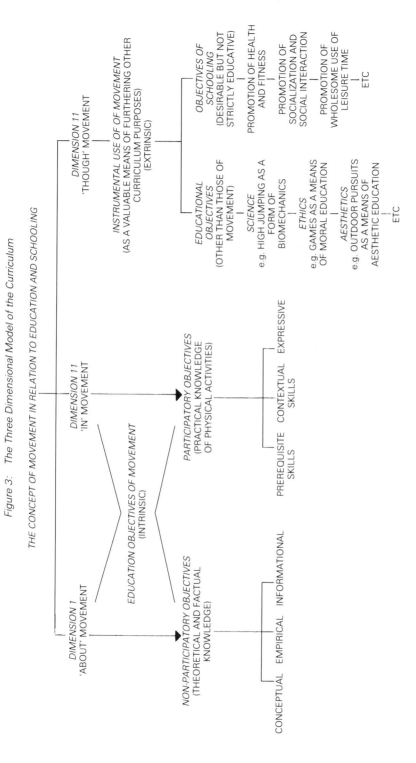

Figure 3: *The Three Dimensional Model of the Curriculum*

THE CONCEPT OF MOVEMENT IN RELATION TO EDUCATION AND SCHOOLING

however, that it is possible to understand a game (for example, rugby) without actually having to play it. To maintain this is not to deny the value and experience of playing it but it is to deny the view that is sometimes expressed that it is first necessary to be a competent participant in a game in order to understand it. There is, of course, a big difference between understanding what is entailed by an activity and successfully being able to participate in it. The gap between the concept of an activity and its successful practice is a considerable one. Whereas the successful practice of an activity involves understanding it will be seen that an understanding on its own does not necessarily guarantee its successful practice. It is then possible to be conceptually educated 'about' different forms of movement activity without necessarily having to engage in them. The point is that one aspect of movement education is to do with conceptual clarification and that this does not necessarily involve being a participant.

It is one objective of movement education to ensure that for each activity selected the rules, both formal and informal, should be learnt and understood. It is only by understanding the rules which govern and regulate an activity that an activity can be intelligently entered into as a participant or meaningfully appraised or appreciated by an observer. Conceptual clarification and understanding is therefore of underlying importance as an objective in the movement curriculum.

Conceptual objectives of the movement curriculum it will be appreciated then are logically bound up with the rules of each activity. Whether or not an activity is understood in terms of its rules can only be checked by putting the pupil into a test situation. In the case of rugby football (A) or basketball (B) respectively, for example, the following questions might be put:

(A) (i)   At a line-out team A threw the ball in but it goes straight to their own side. What by rule are the choices now left open to team B?

   (ii)   Describe two penalty moves that could be used on or near an opposition team's 22 metre line.

(B) (i)   At the beginning of a game how many touches is each player permitted?

   (ii)   Name two types of shot that are used and describe *one* of them.

Empirical objectives

If conceptual objectives are concerned with assisting the pupil to understand better what an activity is and how the rules governing it relate to one another, empirical objectives are more to do with helping the pupil to gather and interpret the facts about physical activities and physical activity. Although the conceptual and empirical are kept separate for purposes of exposition it will be appreciated that there is a close connection between them. In many forms of movement study the empirical is dependent upon the conceptual. Unless, for example, one knows what the shot put in athletics is, and what rules govern and characterize that activity, it would not be possible to investigate it empirically. Unless one is first clear what the rules are and what is permitted and what is proscribed, it would be difficult to establish within what parameters the investigation is to be conducted. If the object of the investigation is to improve performance, then the context of endeavour and what can be done and not done within that context must be clearly understood otherwise whatever is learned or discovered may be invalid.

It will be seen that for empirical objectives to be met it is also necessary to have a grasp of scientific method. At school level this need not involve abstruse and complicated techniques but it should involve an understanding of how to seek answers to certain types of questions that arise in movement that are best approached by a proper use of such procedures as forming a hypothesis, conducting an experiment, making observations, and taking measurements. To learn such procedures with the objective in mind of investigating, for example, the most effective way of throwing the javelin by and through the application of biomechanical principles is but one example of what is meant by an empirical objective. Other forms of empirical objective might relate to investigating such factors as strength, endurance, flexibility and balance in relation to specific tasks or activities, or in gathering data on attitudes towards such issues as sponsorship or apartheid in sport. Although such approaches to finding out 'about' movement are attempted in the preparation of teachers little at present is attempted in this way with pupils in schools. With planning, and the collaboration of colleagues from related teaching areas, there is no reason why this element of movement education should not form a contributory strand to the movement curriculum as well as to its assessment.

Informational objectives
Apart from conceptual and empirical objectives both of which are to do with knowledge and understanding there is a third set of objectives which are parasitic upon the other two and which I shall refer to somewhat loosely as informational objectives.

Informational objectives are not so much to do with *what* different movement activities mean or are; nor are they to do with *how* best to scientifically investigate them with the idea of improving performance or developing understanding in relation to them. Rather they are conerned with the promotion of what might be called 'general movement knowledge' that is of interest and use. If the curriculum is to reflect what is judged to be valuable in the culture of a society then, even in a multicultural society, there is little doubt that movement activities are highly valued by many. Despite this, however, as Thompson pointed out a few years ago (1980, pp.136–41) *the study* of movement activities in many schools, as distinct from their practice, finds virtually no place in the curriculum. Now although in some schools this may no longer be true one reason for this, may have been attributable to the work done on 'worthwhile activities' by RS Peters (1966, pp.144–66) where, as was pointed out earlier, he associated the 'serious' curriculum, with 'intellectual' pursuits rather than with 'practical' ones. Be this as it may, the fact is the study of such categories of physical activities as dance and sport are worthwhile even in Peters' terms, in that they are and can be studied 'seriously' by scholars, be they historians, anthropologists, sociologists, psychologists, physiologists, aestheticians or moral philosophers. Clearly, for example, the growth and development of dance can be of historical, sociological and moral interest, just as the biomechanical and physiological study of sport can be of scientific interest. Despite this neglect to study movement in the recent past, present signs are that this is being rectified. Many of the 'physical education' and 'dance' syllabuses, for example, that have recently been approved by the different examining groups responsible for the new General Certificate of Secondary Education examinations, have elements in them that can be studied as well as performed.

The point is that as social and cultural phenomena both sport and dance are probably more important now as a part of the fabric of Western society than ever before. It therefore seems reasonable that one part of the movement curriculum should be concerned with the provision of information *about* movement if the curriculum as a selection of the culture is to have any meaning at all.

Such topics as the following might be undertaken:

1   The development of sport in Britain from 1800
2   Professional sport in contemporary society
3   Local recreational provision
4   Efficient use of the body, for example, carrying and lifting

5   The effects of exercise
6   Methods of training
7   Sport and politics
8   The Olympic Games
9   The World Cup
10 Twentieth century modern dance

Each of the above topics could, and should, be placed within a coherent framework of study as well as having its own distinctive objectives. At the end of each learning unit such questions as the following might be set:

The Development of Sport in Britain from 1800

   (i)   Name *three* major British sports which derived from the public schools and universities.
   (ii) Which *two* separate bodies have controlled the game of soccer over the past century?
   (iii) Why are there two forms of rugby football played in Great Britain?
   (iv) What measures in recent years have been taken in order to help save first-class cricket?
   (v)   Name *two* major sporting events held in Great Britain each year which are now open to both 'amateurs' and 'professionals'.

Methods of Training

   (i)   What training principle should feature in all strength training programmes?
   (ii) What is an 'isometric contraction'?
   (iii) What is 'fartlek' training?
   (iv) What advantages does 'circuit training' have over other forms of training?

In addition to questions arising from discrete study areas such as those listed it would also be possible to test what *general information* has been transmitted by the use of a multiple choice paper.
   Such questions as the following might be considered:

1   With which English village is the early history of cricket associated?
   A   Nonington
   B   Hambledon

     C   Moreton-in-the-Marsh
     D   Castle Howard
     E   Shelford

2   Which one of the following people is regarded as being the father of the Modern Olympic Games?
     A   Lord Burghley
     B   Avery Brundage
     C   Baron Pierre de Coubertin
     D   Prince Philip
     E   Baron de Rothschild

3   With which of the following ballets do you associate the choreographer Kurt Jooss?
     A   The Firebird
     B   Blood Wedding
     C   Swan Lake
     D   Les Biches
     E   The Green Table

4   Which of the following is black, American and a winner at Wimbledon?
     A   Ashley Cooper
     B   Jimmy Connors
     C   Evonne Goolagong
     D   Arthur Ashe
     E   Virginia Wade

Participatory Objectives

As has been suggested, although it is perfectly possible to have a conceptual understanding of an activity without necessarily having the competence to participate in that activity, it would conversely make little sense to say of a participant in an activity that he 'knows how' to participate but has no grasp of what he is doing. As was seen earlier practical knowledge of an activity involves having a clear understanding of what to do and how to proceed. The successful playing of a game like rugby depends not only upon a clear understanding of the rules which govern it but upon being able to demonstrate practical competency within the parameters of those rules. It is in the getting of pupils to be able to perform successfully within a range of selected activities that the 'in' dimension of the movement curriculum is primarily concerned.

    Broadly speaking, it can be said that the aim of the 'in' dimension of the movement curriculum is to initiate pupils into a balanced selection of their culture's physical activities so that they can satisfyingly participate in them in an intelligent and knowledgeable way. It is because aims on their own lack specificity to give clear guidelines for curriculum planners that objectives as more detailed statements of aims become necessary. It will be appreciated that once a justifiable balance between activities has been decided upon the question of objectives becomes largely a matter of spelling out what must be taught in relation to a given number of activities if the pupil is going to be able to participate successfully in them. The point here is that the objectives of a given activity must logically relate to the nature and purpose of *that* activity. Because each separate activity has its own structural character (and is identified as the one that it is because of this), it will also have its own distinctive objectives. The objectives of a given activity in other words are an intrinsic part part of the makeup and purpose of that activity (see figure 1). It follows, therefore, from this that when one refers to the objectives of the 'in' movement curriculum what one is referring to and trying to pin down, teach and get pupils to learn, are those particular features and properties of those activities which have been selected and justified as forming the curriculum in a given school. It will be seen that a curriculum's selected activities *are* its content and that participatory objectives logically derive from these. It is therefore mistaken to maintain or assume that the selection of objectives is prior to the selection of activities as some curriculum models suggest.[9] To do so is to suggest that the content (or selected activities) is but a means of fulfilling previously specified objectives which are somehow only contingently related to the makeup, nature and purpose of the activities themselves. It is to imply, for example, that in a selected activity like soccer that the game is subservient to the learning of its constituent skills. To put the matter another way, it is to contend that the constituent elements of a game are more important than the game itself. This 'objective *before* content' approach to curriculum planning has the effect of rendering an activity like soccer as but a means in the service and promotion of its component parts. Such a view of rational curriculum planning cannot therefore be accepted for it mistakes the 'whole' for its 'parts'.[10]

Having said something in general about how the objectives of the practical movement curriculum are logically related to the individual nature of each selected activity I want to show now, that because of this, it is possible to speak of three different but related types of 'in' movement objectives.

Education, Movement and the Curriculum

Prerequistite skill objectives

Prerequisite skill objectives in movement are those constituent forms of skilled behaviour which are normally considered preconditions of and necessary to being able to successfully take part in an activity. In soccer, for example, a person who was unable to or is very poor at kicking, trapping, dribbling and passing would not very successfully be able to take part. Similarly in tennis a person who was unable to play a forehand, backhand, nor able to serve and volley could hardly be said to 'know how' to play the game. Such skills as these, which are sometimes called 'basic skills', are both fundamental to, and characteristic of, an activity. They are an inherent part of its makeup and identity. In an important sense they are necessary to a person if he or she is to successfully participate in an activity. It is to the planned and systematic teaching of such skills that I am applying the term prerequisite skill objectives.

If prerequisite skill objectives are looked at in relation to the game of basketball, it will be seen that ball handling, dribbling, footwork and shooting are aspects of the game which can be broken down into units which lend themselves to the specific formulation of objectives. In basketball a prerequisite skill objective refers to a particular form of performative attainment which relates to the playing of the game and which is subject to criterial checks. In getting a pupil to efficiently learn a lay up shot as a prerequisite objective, for example, it is necessary to:

(a) accurately state what the objective is;
(b) describe (and demonstrate) how it is to be realized;
(c) provide supervised practice routines;
(d) check on the results (for example, number of successful attempts out of 10 etc);
(e) use information obtained, if of help, as a guide to modify future practice routines.

In common with what are sometimes called 'prespecified objectives' prerequisite skill objectives are seen firstly, as being concerned with a particular or specific form of attainment. Secondly, they are seen as being performative or behavioural and related to the makeup and purpose of the activity of which it forms a part. Thirdly, because prerequisite skill objectives are specific forms of performative attainment they can frequently be measured or are at least open to quantifiable analysis. It will be seen that in stating a prerequisite objective it is necessary to be able to state unambiguously what the objective is.

128

As Mager (1962, p.16) observes: 'A statement of an objective is useful to the extent that it specifies what the learner must be able to DO or PERFORM when he is demonstrating the mastery of the objective'. Again Popham (1969) emphasizes that: 'A satisfactory ... objective must describe an observable *behaviour* of the learner or a product which is a consequence of learner behaviour.'[11]

In general, prerequisite skill objectives in movement should be seen as useful in the development and acquisition of specific skills that are necessary to a particular activity and which can be practised as units within a larger whole. It should be noted that prerequisite skill objectives are not to be seen as ends or as so many terminal points but as related components that are necessary to a successful engagement in a range of selected activities. What should be made clear is that although the acquisition of basic skills may be necessary to successful participation they are by no means sufficient.

Contextual objectives

Contextual objectives are not so much to do with the acquisition of basic skills in isolation but with their intelligent employment in a given context. They are a good deal more complex than prerequisite objectives in that they cannot so easily be prespecified, practised, measured and assessed. Often in a game, for example, there is always an element of the unpredictable or the unexpected. Performance cannot therefore be programmed in advance. What is required is not a routinized or habitual response but a perceptive and intelligent one. Even so, to a certain extent 'live' situations can be anticipated and practised so that in an actual game, what should be done, can be more readily discerned. Looked at in this way contextual objectives can be seen as various forms of skilled ability which can, in some degree, be planned for and discriminatingly implemented in terms of moves, tactics, ploys and strategies, all of which presuppose a mastery of prerequisite skills. All this can be taught on the basis of: 'given *this* situation *these* responses are often appropriate'. In tennis, for example, it is possible to practise the situation of an opponent advancing to the net in terms of the appositeness of playing:

    (a)   a forehand pass down the line;
    (b)   a backhand cross court drive;
    (c)   a lob over his head.

Such 'situations' as these occur in all sports and can, within limits, be planned for and practiced. Competence is measured in terms of the ability to perfom them in the appropriate circumstances at the right time.

When contextual objectives are seen as 'intended learning outcomes' in the form of contextual abilities which are performed with understanding and discrimination, they should be seen as particular instances of practical reasoning and as exemplifications of an education 'in' movement.

Oldfield (1959) clearly recognizes the relationship between prerequisite and contextual skills when he observes that what is learned in playing tennis is not a set of strokes, but how to make strokes appropriate to the moment.

The point about a skill as a contextual ability is that it is not routinized or subject to prespecification in a narrow, habitual and predictable way but is a form of 'knowing how'. Whereas the learning of basic skills as prerequisite objectives may to some extent demand habituated conformity to a prescribed standard sequence of motor behaviour, the development of skills as acquired contextual abilities are characterized by an intelligent response in the context of the unfolding and living dynamic of the activity. Unlike the somewhat habituated learning routines of basic skill acquisition, contextual skills, as exemplifications of 'knowing how', are characterized by a display of appropriateness of response to a situation as it is encountered. In the context of a game, the skilled performer is recognized by his ability to adapt and adjust, and do the right thing at the right time.

It will be seen that contextual objectives are of a higher order than prerequisite objectives. Whereas the latter are concerned with basic skill acquisition as a precondition of the learning of particular activities, the former are concerned with the development of the standard and quality of engagement in terms of contextual understanding and skill mastery. Skill mastery in fact can be seen as a contextual ability to perform competently and intelligently in the midst of changing circumstances.

Expressive objectives

Expressive objectives differ from prerequisite skill and contextual objectives in that although they have a good deal in common with them in that skills and techniques have to be learned, they are much much more directly concerned with a person's ability to be expressive of a mood, situation or idea as well as with his or her ability to innovate and be imaginative and creative. Clearly 'movement' activities, like mime and dance, by their very nature both demand and provide more scope for the fufilment of expressive objectives than more obviously formalized and rulebound activities such as soccer or hockey.

It should be made clear that when the term 'expressive objective' is used it is not a question of trying to get children to 'give off' or 'give vent' to their feelings as they occur in a naturalistic form as when, for example, they might 'jump for joy', 'shake with fear' or 'sob with disappointment'. Such instances of self-expression may be regarded more as forms of emotional discharge. In contrast, what the expressive objective is seeking in the context of education, is not an uncontrolled 'spewing forth' of feeling, as Dewey (1958, pp.61–2) called it, but a considered and knowledgeable 'working out process' in relation to a given task. In so far as this working out process is 'creative', it is pedagogically sensible to view it, as has been suggested, in terms of a pupils's biography, rather than in terms of cultural uniqueness. If, in common with other objectives, the expressive objective is to be evaluated in terms of its outcomes, it is infinitely more objective to look at what has been produced than an attempt to take account of the psychological processes and experiences involved in that production, important though these may be. As has been said many times before, 'An inner process stands in need of outward criteria'.[12] This observation is particularly pertinent for those teachers who are concerned with how best to evaluate the outcomes of expressive objectives, especially perhaps when they comprise tasks that involve the aesthetic as well as the creative. It is only on the basic of publically-established criteria that the outcome of an expressive objective can be adequately evaluated. The point here is that although an expressive objective might be stated in an open-ended way as 'to stimulate, encourage and develop creative thought and action' in general terms it only begins to make sense when it is seen in the context of an activity, such as dance, where it can be perceived in terms of such criteria as the posing of an unusual problem, an unexpected solution, an inventive use of movement or a distinctive as opposed to clichéd form of communication.

Although expressive objectives set in movement will arise from a given context (for example, gymnastics or dance) and will have (or should have) developed criteria that inherently relate to that context, it will be appreciated that because the outcome is not preconceived or prespecified, it can only be evaluated retrospectively on the basic of what has been accomplished. This is because the nature of an expressive objective 'is evocative rather than prescriptive' (Eisner, 1975, p.353).

Eisner (*ibid*, p.352) speaks of an expressive objective as an 'educational encounter'. He explains:

> The expressive objective is intended to serve as a theme around which skill and understandings learned earlier can be brought to bear, but through which those skills and understandings can be expanded, elaborated, and made idiosyncratic. With an expressive objective what is desired is not homogeneity of response among students but diversity. In the expressive context the teacher hopes to provide a situation in which meanings become personalized and in which children produce products, both theoretical and qualitative, that are as diverse as themselves.

Lastly, Eisner (*ibid*) observes:

> In the expressive context, the product is likely to be as much of a surprise to the maker as it is for the teacher who encounters it.

Lest it should be thought that expressive objectives are only applicable to 'open' situations it should be pointed out that they can apply also to relatively 'closed' and structured ones. It may not be thought possible, for example, for a pupil or pupils to be very 'expressive' when confined to working on two parallel beams, yet in pursuing themes such as symmetry and asymmetry and calling upon a range of mastered skills in the form of upward and downward circles, over and through swings, star shapes, falling leaves and so on, it is possible to compose sequences that demonstrate not only an understanding of the concept involved but innovatory ideas and movements as well as aesthetic sensitivity, all of which can bring about a sense of exploration, achievement and satisfaction.

Examples of expressive objectives in movement are:

1 to work out and perform a new movement sequence on two agility mats calling upon the skills so far learnt and demonstrating a good understanding of such factors as space, weight, time and flow (one, two or three pupils);
2 to mime the situation of an unexpected but happy reunion (two pupils);
3 to create a novel but harmonious sequence in synchronized swimming involving four classmates;
4 to choreograph a dance to a piece of music of your own choosing (solo performance).

Two points need to be emphasized about expressive objectives 'in' movement. The first is that they predominantly, if not exclusively, arise from those forms of activity which are inherently concerned with the promotion of such values and qualities. Whilst all movement activities in one sense allow the person to be self-expressive only some logically demand that the performer be aesthetically expressive. Clearly mime and dance as art forms are among these as are, to a lesser extent, activities like synchronized swimming and some forms of gymnastics and ice-skating. The second point is that because an expressive objective demands some degree of 'openness' and freedom, it should not be thought that the development of appropriate skills and techniques are in any way incompatible with this. Indeed as Best (1979, p.217) has pointed out 'the teaching of techniques, so far from inhibiting or distorting freedom of thought and individual develop-ment, is the only way of making it possible.'

Educational Objectives Summarized

In the light of what has been said the objectives of the 'educational' element of the movement curriculum can be stated as follows:

Non-Participatory

1 to provide a knowledge and understanding of a selected num-ber of physical activities;
2 to promote the ability and confidence to undertake small scale empirical investigations into one or more aspects of human movement studies;
3 to develop an awareness and appreciation of the place of movement in its various forms in culture.

Participatory

4 to perform and analyze skills arising from a balanced selection of activities;
5 to apply these skills successfully and with understanding in context;
6 to provide opportunities for creative composition, expressive action and aesthetic appraisal, particularly in relation to such activities as dance and mime.

Notes

1   See, example, Bloom, *et al* (1966), Krathwohl (1956), Harrow (1972) and Tyler (1971).

What is often meant by Rational Curriculum Planning by Behavioural Objectives (RCPBO) is characterized by four features:

(i)   That education can be defined as *the process of changing behaviour*, or as *changing behaviour*;

(ii) That the ends of the curriculum, generally referred to as objectives, are stated in *behavioural* forms;

(iii) that such objectives *must be measurable*;

(iv) that both the *content* of what is taught and the *method* by which it is taught are seen as *means* to these behavioural, measurable objectives.

For comment on the above see Open University, Unit 16 (1976, pp.23–31)

2   See Oakeshott (1962, pp.198–9).

3   Hirst (1969, p.143), for example, writes that the term applies 'most appropriately to the programme of activities, to the course to be run by pupils in being educated'. It will be recalled, that for Hirst (1974, p.141), education is the 'development of mind' by an initiation into certain forms of intellectual pursuits such as science, mathematics, literature and the fine arts etc. Schooling, on the other hand, is often seen to be a more general term which, takes into account other aspects of a person's welfare such as health. See, for example, Barrow (1981, pp.32–69).

4   Carr (1978), it will be recalled, has argued that practical pursuits, no less than theoretical ones, have their own rationality.

5   For a more complete explication of knowing by acquaintance and its connection with kinaesthetic perception see Arnold (1979b, pp.110–5).

6   A 'core' subject is one of a restricted number of subjects which, it is suggested, should form a necessary part of the curriculum for all pupils. Kirk (1986, p.2) refers to the 'core curriculum' as constituting 'those activities or studies that all pupils will be expected to undertake'. In Scotland the Munn Report (1977) accords physical education this status.

7   See, for example, Maclure (1983) and Skilbeck (1980).

8   Two articles which explore the relationship between the 'intrinsic' and the 'extrinsic' values of physical activities in the context of the school are those by Meakin (1983) and Thompson (1983).

9   Tyler's (1971) original linear model, for example, depicts objectives as preceding content. It thus ran: objectives ... content ... organization ... evaluation.

10 For a further clarification of this issue, especially with regard to the arts, see Stenhouse (1970–71, pp.73–83).

Consult also unit E. 283 of the Open University (1972, pp.96–103).

11 It should be made clear that although I am quoting with approval the wording of these two statements in this context I do not support in general the behaviouristic theory upon which the behavioural objectives 'approach' to education is based. It is too narrow and confining to apply

to educational programmes. In particular it has been criticized as being reductionist, mechanistic and inappropriate to some forms of learning.

For a general discussion on the use of objectives in curriculum planning see Davies (1976).

For a scathing attack on the use of behavioural objectives in education see Bull (1985).

12 See, for example, Wittgenstein (1953, p.153).

10 Curriculum Evaluation and the Role of the Teacher

It has been suggested that a part of rational curriculum planning involves evaluation and that the role of the teacher in this is both central and important. The effectiveness of any planned curriculum programme lies largely in the extent to which the objectives stated are appropriate and realizable by individual children, whether they are taught singly or in groups. What I now want to suggest is that the degree of effectiveness can only be gauged if what is done and what is accomplished in terms of learning outcomes is monitored and appraised in some way. The term for this process is evaluation and it should not be seen as a separate activity from teaching but a necessary and intrinsic part of it. Evaluation, in other words, should be seen as an integral part of professional practice that is consistent with autonomy, responsibility and accountability. What evaluation and accountability should not be seen as (or seen as only) are short-term responses to pupil, parental, administrative or political pressures.

What then is the position of movement with regard to curriculum evaluation? I would say that despite considerable interest and activity in recent years to 'assess' and 'evaluate' 'physical education' programmes in schools the following two general criticisms remain applicable:

1   That there is still conceptual confusion about how to employ the term movement (and/or physical education) and that as a result of this there is a failure to differentiate between (a) those objectives which arise from a study of movement or its practice (non-participatory and participatory respectively) which are 'educative' in nature; and (b) those objectives which are extrinsically directed, such as health or socialization, which, although they are the concern of the movement curriculum, are best regarded as objectives of 'schooling' rather than of education[1].

2   That there is a simplistic view about what evaluation involves. This manifests itself in two main ways:
    (i)   the tendency to think that the answer to problems of evaluation lies only in taking a scientific approach and the possibility of 'measurement';
    (ii) the tendency to be committed to one method of approach (for example, the behavioural objectives model) to the neglect and apposite use of others.

On the first of these general criticisms perhaps enough has already been said[2]. The main point here is that the educational objectives of the participatory movement curriculum arise from the distinctive nature of each and every different selected activity. In other words each activity that forms a part of the participatory dimension of the curriculum has its own objectives. There may be common features and similarities between one activity and another but if they are to remain true to themselves they must be seen and understood in terms of their own 'idiom'. As Oakeshott (1962) has long argued, all action takes place within a specific context and set of conditions. If activities are to be justified in educational terms they must be seen as worthwhile in terms of themselves and not in terms of extrinsic purposes, however desirable. Rational planning (and evaluation) of the movement curriculum must therefore take proper account of the way in which each selected activity characteristically proceeds or should proceed — and all that this implies.

Concerning the second criticism it is now more generally recognized, whether in reference to movement or any other school subject, that evaluation involves a good deal more than just measurement or the use of prespecified behavioural objectives as a basis of appraisal. Indeed both tendencies can be regarded as an attempt to reduce education to a scientific activity. The behavioural categories of the cognitive, the affective and the psychomotor, which are often invoked as an approach to assessment in movement, are as untenable in practice as they are in theory. In brief they are untenable in theory because they rest upon an inadequate view of knowledge. That is to say, instead of seeing knowledge as being concerned with an understanding and practise of distinguishable pursuits and activities, they represent a mechanistic attempt to depict it as so many categorized items of behavioural achievement which, although they may lend themselves to measurement, are in danger of being left unrelated or insensitive to the contextual complexities of a given situation. The corollary of this is that the objectives stated tend to be seen not so much as means but as ends. Insofar as these points relate to movement it will be appreciated that any one activity is more than the parts into which it can be analyzed. Just as a house is more than the materials out of which it is constructed so a game like rugby, for example, is more than its listed patterns of behaviour. In any case the categories are untenable in practice, partially because not all activities predispose themselves to being divided up into artificial and somewhat arbitrarily imposed segments, and partially because, as has been shown, not all learning objectives can be prespecified (for example, expressive objectives), even in principle, for this would deny what a particular activity (for example, creative dance) inherently demands. A further difficulty for the behavioural subjectives approach to curriculum evaluation in general is that it does not always make clear whether the term 'behaviour' just *consists in* what pupils do or whether it is being used as a *criterion* that something is being done with an appropriate appreciation of what is involved.

As Hirst (1974) observes 'states of mind should never be confused with evidence for them' (p.21). This applies as much to 'physical' activities as to 'academic' ones. What appears to be an appropriate action in a movement activity is not necessarily an 'understood' or a 'felt' one. A good mime, for example, will perhaps not only bring spontaneity to what he or she is doing but move with feeling and understanding in the pursuit of his or her art. It is the totality of what is being artistically expressed that is important for purposes of evaluation not its hypothesized and behaviourally prespecified parts. To see a mime or a dance only as a means of bringing about a number of prespecified learning outcomes is not only to put the cart before the horse but is to reduce the intrinsic worth of an activity to a form of instrumentality. All in all, what is being suggested is that not all objectives of the movement curriculum can be prespecified and neither can they be separated out into discrete categories and meaningfully be assessed independently of one another. Any attempt therefore to introduce a behavioural objectives approach to the evaluation of movement should be critically scrutinized for at the end of the day it can be distorting, dehumanizing and reductionist. In short it can be anti-educational.

Perhaps enough has been said to suggest that:

evaluation is a very complex process which is concerned with answering questions of many kinds. Some questions are such that empiricisim cannot provide an appropriate basis for an answer. An evaluation, for example, may include some discussion of the nature and value of the aims of development. Such discussion should be rational, well-informed and conceptually coherent, but it is difficult to see any way in which questions of this sort can be answered by empirical enquiries (Williams, 1981, p.71).

In the light of these general comments and the fact that in the literature there is still considerable bewilderment about movement in relation to curriculum evaluation — what it means, what its purposes are, what form it can take, and what practical suggestions can be made for the teacher, I propose saying something about each of these matters in turn.

The Meaning of Evaluation and Related Terms

Evaluation is an appraisal term to do with the determination of whether or not something is of value. Curriculum evaluation presupposes a sound grasp of the concepts of 'schooling' and 'education' for, as has been shown, their aims and objectives are not necessarily the same. Insofar as evaluation relates to that part of the curriculum that is concerned with education, it is necessarily to do with estimating its effectiveness in terms of the values that the term embodies. If, as has been suggested, education is to be understood as an initiation into those worthwhile pursuits of an 'academic' and 'physical' kind for their own sake and in a morally defensible manner, it will be seen that evaluation entails making judgments not only in relation to the appropriateness of *what* is taught but also about the *manner* in which it is taught. Evaluation in education then, at least at its most basic level, is or should be, concerned with the task of finding out whether or not the content and methods of teaching are satisfactory and, if not, discovering why this is so with the idea in mind of making changes in order to improve them. What it is important to emphasize is that evaluation, as Straughan and Wrigley (1980, p.9) make clear, is allied to the question of values and that it has purpose. In the last analysis evaluation is a value judgment about what is happening or has happened and what, if necessary, should be done about it.

What seems clear is that evaluation is a broader term than either assessment or measurement. Whereas *assessment* is essentially concerned with the cultivation and refinement of techniques (tests and examinations, etc) for the collection and provision of appropriate data upon which judgments can be made, *measurement* is essentially concerned with the presentation of that evidence in quantifiable form. Measurement, in other words, can be considered as one approach to assessment that characteristically expresses its results in terms of numbers. It should be stressed that measurement is not appropriate to all aspects of the movement curriculum even though it may be appropriate to some. It would be foolish, for example, to attempt to measure the worth of a dance. Although measurement implies quantification and objectivity it should not be thought, as some social scientists do, that it is necessary to measure something in order to be objective about it. As Best (1980) and others have pointed out, it is possible to be objective in the arts no less than in the sciences. The point is that it is reductionist to understand 'objectivity' only in empirical or scientible terms.

What movement, no less other subjects in the curriculum should be safeguarded against is the mistaken belief that complex human actions and activities can be reduced to or evaluated only by reference to 'intervention-counts and test responses'.[4] Measurement, it should be understood, is a servant not master of any attempt to evaluate educational programmes.

If evaluation is to be of help to the movement curriculum and its development it must be seen as a process which makes use of reliable and valid assessment techniques, which provide both *qualitative* as well as *quantitative* information about either a process or a product which can be seen to be of use by the practising teacher. In short the effective teacher of movement activities needs to develop a full range of evaluative skills ranging from forms of measurement to more complex forms of observation and illuminative procedures.[5]

In attempting to provide a conceptual framework for evaluation Sockett (1979, p.9) identifies four central features. They are, I think, particularly apposite to what has so far been argued about the nature of movement activities, what their objectives should be, and how best to approach them in terms of evaluation. They are as follows:

  (i)   evaluation is appraisal in which we make judgments;
  (ii) such judgments are made in the light of criteria;
  (iii) criteria issue from, and are appropriate to, particular contexts;
  (iv) such contexts embody human purposes, and evaluations made therefore inform decisions.

What is at the heart of this account of the meaning of evaluation is that each activity can only be judged in terms of what it is; in terms of its own internal logical structure. In so far as the 'participatory objectives' of movement are concerned they are what they are because each activity is what it is. What is accomplished with reference to each activity is judged 'good' or 'bad' in terms of its own criteria of what is good or bad. Cricket is judged according to the canons of cricket; rugby according to the canons of rugby. There are no general canons by which movement as a whole family of different activities can be judged, for each activity is judged in accordance with its own distinctive character. Curriculum evaluation in movement, especially its educational aspects, only makes sense as long as this is borne in mind.

At the end of the day it should not be forgotten that for the practising teacher the prime purpose of evaluation is to facilitate rational decisions in the attempt to improve pupil learning.

The Purposes of Evaluation

If evaluation can be accepted as being concerned with the process of delineating and obtaining pertinent evidence for the making of judgments and the choosing between possible alternatives about what it is best to do it raises the further question 'for what types of particular decision?' Cronbach (1963) lists three major forms of consideration:

(i) Course improvement: deciding which instructional material and methods are satisfactory and which are in need of change.

(ii) Decisions about individuals: identifying the needs of each pupil for the sake of planning his or her instruction, judging pupil merit for the purposes of selection and grouping, acquainting the pupil with his or her own progress and deficiencies.

(iii) Administrative regulation: judging how good the school system is, how good individual teachers are, and so on.

Traditionally the teacher of movement activities has been concerned with the first two of these categories where considerations of *what* to teach, and *how* best to teach it are borne in mind. More recently, however, especially since the notion of accountability has gathered force[6], the third category has had increasing implications for the teacher compelling him to think not only what he is doing and how he is doing it but *why* he is doing it. Coupled with the demand for accountability, and perhaps underlying it, is the question of standards and what levels of achievement can be reasonably expected for given groups of children at various ages and stages.[7] What needs to be understood in the present context, as was hinted at earlier, is that if evaluation is carried out intelligently as a part of responsible professional practice, it will provide the rational basis for what it is to be accountable.[8] I do not propose here to take this point further but instead concentrate upon six purposes of evaluation each of which are of immediate interest to the practising teacher and which in turn relate, directly or indirectly, to each of the three categories previously listed. The six purposes of evaluation I propose to outline are: programme selection; knowledge appraisal; diagnosis and guidance; motivation; classification and grading; efficacy of teaching.

Programme Selection

The question of what is taught and why it is taught should always be a matter of monitoring and review otherwise what is chosen will become merely a matter of tradition and ritual.[9] No hard and fast list of activities can or should be laid down other than to say that in the interests of balance the teacher should bear in mind not only the underlying considerations of rational curriculum planning (see figure 1, chapter 9) but the varying claims of such groups of activities as gymnastics, field games, court games, dance, swimming, athletics and outdoor pursuits. In the presentation of these, one form of vertical and horizontal planning of the curriculum may prove to be more helpful to teaching and learning than another.

Knowledge Appraisal

As has been made clear, once the selection of activities has taken place evaluation becomes very much a question of 'To what extent have the objectives arising from the inherent structure of those activities been realized?' One purpose of evaluation therefore is to provide an answer to this question in terms of what type of knowledge has been gained. Here the familiar distinction between 'knowing-that' and 'knowing-how' applies. The former is concerned with assessing the extent to which an activity (or number of activities) is understood by a knowledge of its rules, techniques, strategies, etiquette etc. The emphasis in this type of knowledge is on what can correctly be said or written about such matters. The latter is concerned with assessing whether such understandings are being successfully implemented in practice in terms of the performance of basic skills, contextual abilities, strategic ploys, and choreographic presentation. If there is a gap between what is understood and what is performed then it becomes a matter of judgment as to what can or should be done about it.

It will be clear then that movement as a part of the general curriculum of the school can be academically studied in addition to being performed. Both ways of knowing can be assessed with the intention of improving each.

In order to illustrate more fully what is possible here two examinations will be referred to. Both are at General Certificate in Secondary Education (GCSE) level and have therefore been devised for pupils of approximately 16 years of age. The first concerns the subject of 'physical education' in which the Northern Examining Board state one of the main aims as being 'To increase the candidate's knowledge, understanding and performance of physical activities'. In turn the 'assessment objectives', which the candidate is expected to meet, are to:

1 demonstrate competence in the chosen physical activities as specified in the subject content;
2 display, as appropriate, a knowledge and understanding of the laws, rules, techniques, strategies and safety factors relating to chosen sports or physical activites;
3 display a knowledge and understanding of the physical basis of performance and exercise in physical activities;
4 display a knowledge of the organization of sports and physical activities in this country and of the social influences on participation;
5 demonstrate the skills of research, analysis and evaluation within a selected area of physical education.

The scheme of assessment accords 50 per cent of the marks to 'practical performance' (objectives 1 and 2) which involves four chosen physical activities; 30 per cent to the 'written paper' (objectives 3 and 4), which consists of both a number of short answer questions as well as free response questions; and 20 per cent to the 'personal study' (objective 5) which involves writing up to 1500–2000 words on an approved topic such as 'the effects of exercise on heartrate' or 'a study of diet and energy expenditure'.

The second examination concerning the subject of 'dance' has been devised by the London and East Anglian Examining Group. The aim is stated as being 'to develop knowledge of dance as an art form'. The 'assessment ojectives' of the examination are to assess the candidate's ability to:

(a)   Choreograph: demonstrate an understanding of choreography through the presentation of their own composition;

(b)   Perform: demonstrate bodily competence and interpretative skills through the performance of dances and studies;

(c)   Appreciate: (i) demonstrate a critical understanding of choreography; (ii) demonstrate a critical understanding of a set work; and (iii) demonstrate an awareness and understanding of broad choreographic trends within an historical context.

The 'scheme of assessment' in relation to these objectives give 50 per cent of the marks to 'practical choreography and performance', which involves composition as well as performance; 30 per cent to 'written appreciation', which is concerned with a knowledge and understanding of broad choreographic trends in a historical context; and 20 per cent to 'course work', which can be on such themes as 'romantic ballet', 'the structure of music and its relationship to dance', 'parallelism and Nijinsky' and 'jazz practical'.

Both these examinations have been singled out for two reasons. The first is that they exemplify and reinforce a point made earlier to the effect that the 'educational' objectives of the movement curriculum should arise from the study and practice of movement. The second reason for outlining the objectives and assessment procedures of these examinations is that they do not, as is sometimes the case, call upon a behavioural objectives model format whereby what is done is arbitrarily split up into the 'cognitive', the 'affective' and the 'psycho-motor' in an artificially divisive and fragmentary way.[10]

In short both these examinations are appropriate, and therefore to be commended from the educational point of view, because they base what they propose to assess on the objectives which arise from the study and practice of movement activities and not upon other extrinsic considerations, such as the furtherance of 'socialization' or 'health', even though these may still come about as fortuitous outcomes.

Diagnosis and Guidance

The evaluation of a pupil's progress will sometimes reveal particular weaknesses or difficulties and once identified a decision can be made about what best to do about them. Remedial treatment in the form of special attention or coaching is often the answer. Sometimes, however, because of something like congenital disability there may be no easy answer. What evaluation often brings to light is the pupil with distinctive interests, personality characteristics, needs and abilities and the decision has to be made as to whether these can be accommodated in some way. Ideally, the curriculum should be as 'individualized' and 'personalized' as possible so that each pupil can be assisted to actualize his potentialities in terms of both education and schooling. In the last resort it is to these considerations to which all teaching should be directed.

Motivation

It is a mute point as to whether or not evaluation should be used as a form of motivation. The fact, however, is that it often acts as one whether it is intended or not.

What is known is that a 'knowledge of results' often acts as a spur to learning.[11] If pupils are encouraged to contract and keep a cumulative profile or record of their progress or otherwise in such matters as 'knowledge of rules' or 'skill acquisition' or in such a domain as athletics, for example, it can lead to a valuable form of *self-evaluation* whereby it becomes evident to them what areas of their profile could be strengthened and need to be improved upon.

Classification and Grading

Evaluation is sometimes used for classification and grading. Classification or the arrangement of pupils into categories or groups can be done for a variety of purposes. The most common and most easily justifiable one is to bring about more effective learning opportunities.

It is more often argued that teaching pupils in comparable ability groups is a more effective way of bringing about intended learning outcomes than if teaching is done in mixed ability groups. If this is so, and forms of assessment can be devised to enable this to be done in a valid and reliable manner, then they can provide a useful service.

Linked to the question of classification is the question of grading. As with other subject areas in education the question of whether or not it is desirable to assign grades is a debatable point and is an issue I do not intend to enter into here. The fact is that evaluation is sometimes used for the purpose of grading and the justification or otherwise of doing it very much depends upon the reasons offered and on how responsibly the results are used. If grades are to relate strictly to how well a pupil has progressed in each of the selected activities of the movement curriculum and not be confused with such other important but often not directly related points of overall concern such as 'social awareness', 'general physical development', 'self awareness', 'enjoyment' or 'cooperation', the following questions should pertain:

(i) What are the inherent objectives of the activity?

(ii) Were the students taught in accordance with these objectives?

(iii) Does the form of assessment (whether tests, examinations, or informed judgments) suitably relate to the objectives in question?

Efficacy of Teaching

The evaluation of pupils can often serve as a form of self-evaluation for the teacher. Test and examination results, apart from providing a basis for monitoring pupil progress, can often be of use in allowing the teacher to appraise his own performance in relation to the suitability and presentation of activities. As a result of looking at the 'results' of a course or an educational programme, the teacher may find it helpful to ask himself such questions as 'Were the activities selected the most appropriate?', 'Was I as clear and as realistic as I might have been in the setting of particular tasks?' 'In what ways can my organization and teaching methods be improved?' How can I bring about greater cooperation and improved forms of communication?'

The active and reflective teacher can learn as much about himself and his teaching skills in the assessment of pupils as he does about them.

Forms of Assessment

It is generally recognized that there are two main approaches to the asessment and testing of children. The first has come to be known as 'norm-referenced', the second a 'criterion-referenced'. Teachers in fact have been using both forms for many years but it is only recently that a formal distinction has been made between them. The difference between one and the other lies mainly in their respective purposes and the types of philosophy they embody. Since both are of interest to the teacher of movement activities I shall outline each in turn.

Norm-Referenced Assessment

Norm-referenced assessment essentially consists in comparing a pupil's attainment with that of others. Its purpose is to make comparison between pupils and to relate these to the average of performances of a large number of similar children (Satterly, 1981, p 54). The 'norm' refers to the norm associated with a particular group no matter what its size and the assessment refers to how well or badly an individual is doing in relation to that group. A person graded as 'A', for example, in terms of the group norm might be described as 'outstanding', whereas another might be graded as 'C' and seen as 'average' and so on. The value of norm-referenced assessment, especially if the test or examination scores have been based on a large population and 'standardized', is that it can indicate the *relative* standing of a pupil within any activity or unit of study for which information from the group performance is available. It can be of use in such matters as 'motivating', 'grading', 'selecting' and 'predicting' if these are thought helpful in some way. For teachers, no less than for research workers and administrators, the availability of school, regional or national norms can provide not only information for purposes of curriculum evaluation and development but also for purposes of accountability.

A general criticism that is sometimes levelled at normative-based asssessment procedures, especially if the group is small and scores unstandardized, is that although they provide a picture of a pupil's standing *relative* to the performance of others in a group, it is of little interest compared with knowledge of the extent to which a learner's attainment approaches a given standard of performance in a particular activity. To say that a pupil is the 'best' in a 'poor' group is not to say much about what level of achievement has been reached. The best swimmer in a group of beginners says little about how well he or she is able to swim. As Brown (1981) says: 'normative scores will not tell us precisely what the pupil knows and can do; they will only tell us whether he or she knows more (or less) and can do more (or less)' (p.1) in relation to others in the same group.

Two particular deficiencies of norm-referenced tests when used to educational purposes are:

(i)   that they do not reveal what knowledge or skill has been achieved in relation to a particular activity, course or unit of work;

(ii)   that they rarely provide an adequate diagnosis of the learning difficulty or shortcoming to be of help to the teacher or pupil.

It is because of these limitations that interest has been shown recently in the development of the second or criterion referenced approach to assessment.

Criterion-Referenced Assessment

Criterion-referenced forms of assessment have been developed in response to norm-referenced forms of assessment not only because of the limitations of the latter in terms of 'objective' information provided but also in an effort to dampen down an undesirable competitive spirit which they sometimes foster.

The purpose of the criterion-referenced approach is to assess the *achievement* of pupils relative not to one another but to an established criterion or standard of performance. It aims to identify what a person knows or is competent in. It is concerned not with how a person stands in relation to others but rather how he or she stands in relation to a knowledge of the subject or how well he or she performs in relation to a particular activity. As Brown (*ibid* p.14) puts it:

> Criterion referenced assessment provides information about the specific knowledge and abilities of pupils through their performances on various kinds of tasks that are interpretable in terms of what the pupils know or can do, without reference to the performance of others. (p.14)

Criterion referencing can therefore be of great value in analyzing the strengths and weaknesses of a particular pupil in relation to a skill or standard of performance. A criterion-referenced test is often referred to as one that is 'used to ascertain the degree of correspondence between the performance or learning by an individual and a precise definition of the behaviour exhibited by a 'successful' learner of a well defined objective for learning' (Satterly, 1981, p.348). Frequently such tests cover relatively small units of content (for example, a head spring or a shot put or tennis serve) and the scores are interpreted as showing what the individual learner can do rather than serve as a *comparison* with other individuals. A criterion-referenced score indicates the level of a pupil's achievement (or otherwise) in relation to an objective or a necessary and constituent part of an activity. It should be noted that when the term 'criterion' is used to define a level of performance reached it does not refer to an end behaviour but rather to a difference in standard along an achievement continuum. Criterion-referenced measures or grades thus provide information about the degree of competence attained by a particular pupil which is independent of reference to the performance of others. It should be pointed out, however, that criterion-referenced and norm-referenced approaches to assessment are not always as mutually exclusive as they are sometimes presented as being. Barrow (1984, p.236) points to the illogicality of this position. In the school situation it is not easy to see how criterion-referenced assessment can ever be entirely disassociated from norm-referencing for in order to decide upon what criteria to use it is necessary first to know what pupils can reasonably be expected to achieve at different ages or levels of development. Taken together the two approaches should be seen as different but complementary. Whereas the norm-referenced approach helps in the identification of *relative* performance and is therefore able to indicate who is likely to need remedial work or 'individually guided education', the criterion-referenced approach is better from the diagnostic point of view in that it is better able to identify what *actual* strengths or weaknesses in a performance are present and is therefore likely to be more helpful in deciding upon what should be taught in the future if a given standard of performance is to be achieved.

Formative and Summative Evaluation

Two types of evaluation linked to criteria and norm referencing respectively are formative and summative. *Formative evaluation* is that which takes place during the teaching-learning process with the idea of identifying weaknesses in pupil performance and correcting them with respect to a particular course or unit of work. It is ongoing, diagnostic and is an integral part of the lesson or programme whilst it is in operation. The purpose of formative evaluation is not so much to judge but to improve what is being attempted by intelligently monitoring what is going on and how this is helping or otherwise to meet the objectives that have been set. In order to do this effectively it will be seen that the criteria by which the objectives are identified have to be borne clearly in mind. If one method of teaching is proving ineffectual it may be necessary to switch to another. *Formative evaluation*, whether in the form of perceptive observation or test scores, should be a part of the teacher's everyday business.

Summative evaluation is not so much concerned with the provision of 'feedback' in order to help individual pupils in an ongoing way but with the overall effectiveness or otherwise of a programme after it has been completed. Apart from reflecting on the achievements of pupils relative to one another, it can be used to determine pupil grades with the idea of placing them in more effective learning groups. In addition, however, summative evaluation should be concerned with whatever information is required about intended as well as unintended outcomes and try to appraise the worth or desirability of each. Only by doing so is it possible to decide whether or not, the grogramme can be altered, modified and improved. As Luff (1980) observes: 'If summative evaluation measures only the degree to which goals or objectives have been met, then it is likely to be somewhat narrow and introspective, and accepting of the values rather than questioning them . . .' (p.20).

In summary it can be said that whereas formative evaluation is carried out primarily by and for those who are teaching and developing a particular curriculum programme or course, summative evaluation is carried out more often by those not directly involved in the development. Although at present this may be the fact of the matter, I would suggest, that, in future, the practising teacher should be involved in both forms of evaluation, for it is often the case that the results or 'feedbark' arising from summative forms of evaluation have implications for future formative forms of evaluation. Again the one is often complementary to the other.

Standards, Grade Related Criteria, Profiling and GCSE Certification

Associated with the question of assessment is the question of 'standards'. Broadly speaking the idea of a standard is that it is an approved or accepted example of something against which others are measured or judged. In this sense it serves as a model of attainment or performance for purposes of measurement, comparison, or aspiration.

The practical question for the teacher, however, is not so much what a standard is but how can standards in schools be set? Glass (1978) presented a number of ways through which this problem can be considered. Only two of them will be mentioned here. The first is by studying the performance of a large number of comparable children. This clearly is in keeping with the norm-referenced approach. In order to determine what a reasonable level of expectation is the *median* score for pupils of the 'same type' is taken as the single most useful reference point for establishing a basis for assessment. Clearly if something like National Standard Scales were available for such obviously 'measurable' activities as athletics and swimming, they could act as an important reference for one approach to assessment. If it was known, for example, that the 'average' 15 year-old boy was able to long jump 15'6" it would provide a good indicator of what could reasonably be expected and a grading scale worked out accordingly.

The second way of how standards can be set is to study the performance of established 'masters' (ie. expert performers). Here the standards (and qualities) recognizable in the masterly performance are taken as the criteria against which other judgments are made. This approach to the problem of standards is in keeping with the criterion-referenced approach to assessment. It has the merit of not only focussing upon what is entailed by the nature of the activity rather than just on its 'result' but permits a greater appreciation of what is possible. Furthermore it will be seen that the notion of criteria goes far beyond the concept of measurement. It is concerned more with being able to identify and understand what is being attempted so that judgments can be made in relation to it. Thus, once the criteria of a particular activity have been made clear by a study of it in relation to its master performers, whether gymnast, athlete or dancer, it becomes more possible to appraise it in a knowledgeable and educated way. To understand and appreciate an activity by the criteria that both characterizes and governs it is to be educated in the ways of that activity. It is only when this is understood can a proper evaluation of it take place. In this sense it can be said that the identifiable criteria of an activity are also its objectives and it is to these one should look in making a judgment. The great exponents of particular activities are the highest standard bearers of those activities. It is to them that assessors should look in the first place for the setting of a supreme standard against which all other standards are related whether they are concerned with such procedures as 'counting back from 100 per cent' or gauging what something like 'minimal competency' is.

In the new General Certificate of Secondary Education (GCSE) examinations in England and Wales, which apply to pupils who have spent four years in secondary schools and who are approximately 16 years of age, the policy of grading by criterion-referencing has been adopted for some twenty subjects. Grading here means the system under which grades are defined and awarded in terms of predetermined standards of performance specific to the subject concerned. A seven-point scale has been adopted denoted by the letters A,B,C, D,E,F,G. [12] A candidate who fails to meet the minimum standards for grade G will receive no certificate in that subject. It is of interest to note that physical education and dance are not among those twenty subjects that *have* to produce 'subject specific criteria' but are included amongst those subjects which *may* be examined provided they conform to the 'general criteria'. In this context general criteria means the submission of a subject syllabus which includes the following elements:

1 Title
2 Statement of general aims
3 The assessment of objectives
4 The proportion of marks allocated to each objective
5 The scheme of assessment
6 The subject content
7 Grade descriptions for at least grades C and F.

It is of interest to note that provided each of the five regionally-based examining groups[13] keep within the above guidelines what is actually done can vary.

Although in physical education and dance 'grade descriptions', or the attempt to describe in positive and subject specific terms the expected level of attainment, are only required for examination purposes for grades C and F, ideally they should ultimately be worked out if possible along the whole seven-point scale continuum for each separate activity, on a grade-related criteria' or 'grade criteria' basis if the principle of *differentiation* is to be achieved.[14] In fact, some regions have already seen the need to take things beyond that which is at present required. The Northern Examining Association, for example, has worked out in the case of ten physical activities 'grade descriptions'of competence on a five-point scale. The two on the next page refer to badminton and hockey.

Whether, in fact, with the passage of time it will prove possible or desirable to work out in a reliable and valid way on a seven-point scale national grade criteria for each physical activity taught in the secondary school remains to be seen. In principle, at least, it seems the logical and sensible thing to try to do.

What clearly seems desirable, not only for purposes of certification but for evaluating the progress of all pupils, is the keeping of an individual record or *profile* report. This would not only be of pedago-

(a) Badminton

Level	Description
5	Difficulty in performing even the very basic strokes of the game.
4	Ability to demonstrate individual strokes, without an ability to prolong a rally or make attacking shots.
3	Ability to play a game of singles and/or doubles using only the basic strokes and involving only short rallies. Ability to keep score throughout the game.
2	Ability to produce correct strokes, as above, but in practice and during a normal game, as opposed to the pressures of match play. Basic knowledge of tactics and the ability to implement them in both singles and doubles play. Ability to keep the score throughout the game and have some knowledge of setting.
1	Ability to play and produce the correct tactical strokes in a match situation. Both singles and doubles competence is expected and an awareness of court positioning of oneself and one's opponent(s) is essential. Ability to play all strokes, including the smash and drop shot. To score throughout the game, showing an understanding of setting.

(b) Hockey

Level	Description
5	Difficulty in performing even the basic skills of pushing and hitting and in stopping a ball. Inability to relate personal performance to team play and having little knowledge of the rules.
4	Ability to play a game whilst showing some evidence of skills relative to an individual position but not always possessing the control to make a positive contribution to team play. Some knowledge of rules as evidenced in a game situation.
3	Ability to show good individual skills relative to an individual position, but showing a rather inconsistent execution of technique. A sound knowledge of the rules of the game accompanied by an understanding of basic tactics and strategies to be employed in team play.
2	Ability to play a significant role in a competitive game at a good level relative to one's age-group. Ability to show the full range of skills in relation to an individual position whilst not always relating these to the 'reading' of the game. Evidence of both application of rules and awareness of tactics and strategies necessary for successful team play.
1	Ability to play a competitive game at a high level relative to one's age-group. Ability to show the full range of strokes, including the scoop, within the game, having understanding and 'vision' in respect to an individual position. Ability to fulfil positional requirements with flexibility to change roles depending upon situation. Evidence of both an advanced knowledge of the rules and their application. An awareness of tactics and strategies necessary for successful team play.

gic value to the teacher but would be a source of information to the parent or future employer about what a particular pupil knows or can do. Ideally in a subject area such as movement a profile booklet should reflect not only a balance between 'theory' and 'practice', in the way outlined in the last chapter (see figure 3 p.121), but between 'examination' and 'course work'. Although it may not be able to document accurately a pupil's progress, or otherwise, in relation to all that is implicit in the movement curriculum in terms of education or schooling (especially perhaps in the moral and aesthetic spheres), it should be possible to devise a system of assessment profiling in such areas as 'Knowledge and understanding', 'Practical performance' and 'Critical evaluation'. It is often in the 'course work' element, where there is the opportunity to undertake extended pieces of work of either a 'practical' or 'theoretical' nature, that educational aims and objectives can be more fruitfully realized, rather than in the examination element where time is necessarily at a premium. What weighting for purposes of Certification should be given to 'course work' as opposed to 'examinations' is a matter of judgment but at CCSE level there does not seem any good reason why it should not be up to the order of 50 per cent. What a good assessment pattern and profile ought to provide is a picture of *'differentiation'*: that is, it should reveal, not only between different subjects but within each subject, what a particular pupil can do and understand in relation to his or her individual level of ability. What from the evaluative point of view should be resisted (despite it being of understandable convenience to any future employer) is the reduction of the profile, even for certification purposes, to a *'summated grade'*, for it will be seen that one overall grade will not reveal useful data about an individual's strengths and weaknesses.

The Advantages and Disadvantages of National Criteria

Relative to issues concerning standards and certification is the question of whether or not a national system of grade criteria for each and every subject taught in secondary schools is in principle a good thing. Those that argue it is point to two advantages. The first is that it will bring agreement about the essence of what should be taught. This will ensure that the content and objectives of the subject will be nationally determined. This, in turn, it is argued, will bring about the following benefits:

1 Syllabuses for certification purposes can be planned on the firm expectation that pupils in other parts of the country will be covering the same ground. This will enable pupils transferring from one school to another to do so without undue difficulty.

2 Certificates issued will be more useful to employers and others since the grades acquired in a particular subject will

indicate that specific knowledge, skills and competencies have been acquired which have country-wide recognition.

The second main advantage suggested is that good curriculum and assessment practice will be encouraged in that teachers will need to keep abreast with current thinking with regard to both subject content and teaching methods. This, to some extent, will be ensured by the fact that:

(a)   grades will be awarded by adopting a common scale using grade descriptions for guidance;

(b)   there will be common approaches to the moderation of teachers' assessments so that greater objectivity can be achieved.

Those, on the other hand, who argue in principle that the adoption of a national criteria for all subjects taught in secondary schools is a disadvantage, make two main points. The first is that there is danger of central control being imposed on the curriculum. This danger is likely to be exacerbated by the fact that the curriculum will no longer lie with the teacher, the school or the local education authority. Instead the curriculum will be decided, at least partially, by a document formulated in association with, and approved by, the Government.

The second point is that such a move could act as the enemy of innovation and lead to the ossification of the curriculum. It will be seen that this second point relates to the one made above in that on the face of it professional autonomy and the freedom to experiment are likely to be undermined. The curriculum and the individual subject areas that comprise it are, especially over a period of time, likely to be adversely affected. Clearly if this disadvantage is to be offset there must be some built in safeguards that ensure that change can be brought about.[15]

Curriculum Evaluation: A Teacher's Check List

It will have been made clear that curriculum evaluation demands a thorough understanding of *what* is being attempted, *how* it is being attempted, and *why* it is being attempted. It demands that the teacher be fully acquainted amongst other things with the distinctive structure of each activity as well as a sound knowledge of how best to go about appraising what is being done or what has been accomplished. The following is a proposed check list for the practising teacher.

1 Is there a clearly written *rationale* of the proposed programme or unit of work indicating its underlying educational philosophy?

2 Upon what basis has the *selection* of activities or units of work taken place? Is it justifiable?

3 Are the *objectives* of each activity or unit of work selected stated with as much precision as possible?

4 Is the *criteria* for making an assessment with regard to each activity or unit of work clear?

5 Has the problem of what *standards* to adopt been satisfactorily resolved?

6 Are the *tasks and methods* appropriate to the needs, ability and interests of the pupils?

7 Are the *facilities and equipment* necessary to the fulfilment of the programme available?

8 Is there a *system* for the recording of information, providing feedback to the pupils, and reappraising what should be done in the light of what becomes known about both intended as well as unintended outcomes?

9 Has a clear and well-structured *profile report* on each pupil been prepared? Is it able to provide an accurate summary of a pupil's achievements in each activity or area of the curriculum completed?

Notes

1 This is well illustrated in the review of teacher's objectives made by Kane (1974). See chapter 1.
  This lack of differentiation between the objectives of 'education' and 'schooling' is also apparent in a number of the 'physical education' syllabuses that have been recently been approved for the newly introduced General Certificate of Secondary Education.

2 Refer to chapter 8.

3 For a more detailed criticism of the behavioural objectives approach to learning and assessment see Stenhouse (1978, pp.70–83), Sockett (1976, pp.44–51), Kelly (1982, pp.99–108), Hirst (1974, pp.16–29), and White (1971, pp.109–12).

4 See Holt (1981, p26) on what he calls 'technological rationalism'.

5 See Partlett and Hamilton (1975, p.88). The primary concern of illuminative evaluation is with description and interpretation rather than with measurement and prediction.

6 See Sockett (1980, p.9)

7 It is of interest to record that the main purpose of the Assessment of

Performance Unit (APU), which was set up by the Department of Education and Science in 1975, is to devise ways of assessing, in very broad terms, the effectiveness of the educational system by monitoring pupils performance across the curriculum of different stages. Six dimensions of development were hypothesized: mathematical, linguistic, scientific; aesthetic; physical; personal and social. Regrettably in the last three of these areas nothing much of practical consequence has been accomplished. For a background on the APU see Skilbeck (1984, pp.124–64).

8 See Simons (1981).

9 As depicted in 'The saber-tooth curriculum' consult Benjamin (1971, pp.7–9).

10 See for example, the document published by the Scottish Central Committee in Physical Education called *A Framework for Assessment*, (1985, p.13)

11 There are many useful books on this topic in relation to physical activities. See, for example, those by Sage (1984) and Singer (1980).

It should also be remembered that a knowledge of results in the form of comparative marks, can lead to social division which is inimical to a good learning climate. See Satterly (1981, p.48).

12 It is this 'grade criteria' approach to assessment that has now been officially adopted in England and Wales as well as in Scotland, as the way forward in an effort to improve standards as well as to present more clearly what a pupil is capable of doing in relation to the different subject areas of the curriculum. In general 'grade criteria' may be regarded as a form of grading by reference to criteria that reflects a pupil's achievement in relation to a subject, a particular activity, or unit of work.

In a speech at Sheffield in 1984 Sir Keith Joseph, the Secretary of State for Education and Science, called for 'Clear definitions of the knowledge of level and performance expected from candidates for the award of particular grades'.

13 The GCSE will be administered in England and Wales by five examining groups. These are: The London and East Anglian Group; Midland Examining Group; Northern Examining Association; Southern Examining Group; and the Welsh Joint Education Committee.

14 A differentiated examination is one in which different components are deliberately set at different levels of difficulty to meet the needs of candidates of different levels of ability.

15 In England a *National Curriculum Council* will keep curriculum programmes and attainment targets under review, while a *School Examination and Assessment Council* will review assessment procedures and examinations and arrange for the moderation of assessment.

Bibliography

ANDERSON, R.H., LAWSON, R.L., SCHELL, R.L. and SWIFT, D.F. (1968) *Foundation Disciplines and the Study of Education*, Toronto, Macmillan.

ANSCOMBE, G.E.M. (1957) *Intention*, Oxford, Blackwell.

ARISTOTLE, *Ethics*, translation of Nichomachean Ethics by THOMPSON, J.A.K. (1973), London, Penguin.

ARNOLD, P.J. (1973) 'Education and the concept of movement', *Bulletin of Physical Education*, 9, 5, January, pp.13–22.

ARNOLD, P.J. (1979a) 'Intellectualism, physical education and self-actualization', *Quest*, 31, 1, pp.87–96.

ARNOLD, P.J. (1979b) *Meaning in Movement, Sport and Physical Education*, London, Heinemann.

ARNOLD, P.J. (1979c) 'Agency, action and meaning in movement: An introduction to three new terms', *Journal of the Philosophy of Sport*, Fall, pp.49–57.

ARNOLD, P.J. (1980) 'Movement, physical education and the curriculum', *Physical Education Review*, 3,1, spring, pp.14–17.

ARNOLD, P.J. (1982) 'Competitive games and education', *Physical Education Review*, 5, 2, pp.126–30.

ARNOLD, P.J. (1984a) 'Sport, moral education and the development of character', *Journal of the Philosophy of Education*, 18, 2.

ARNOLD, P.J. (1984b) 'Three approaches towards an understanding of sportsmanship', *Journal of the Philosophy of Sport*, 10, pp.61–70.

ASPIN, D. (1975) 'Ethical aspects of sports and games', *Proceedings of the Philosophy of Education Society of Great Britain*, IX, July.

AUSUBEL, D.P. and FLOYD, G.R.(1969) *School Learning*, Holt, Rinehart & Winston.

BAILEY, C. (1975) 'Games, winning and education', *Cambridge Journal of Education*, 5, 1, Lent, pp.40–50.

BAILEY, C. (1984) *Beyond the Present and Particular*, London, Routledge & Kegan Paul.

BANTOCK, G.H. (1971) 'Towards a theory of popular education' in HOOPER, R. (Ed) *The Curriculum, Context, Design and Development*, Edinburgh, Oliver & Boyd.

BARROW, H.M. (1983) *Man and Movement: Principles of Physical Education,* Philadelphia, PA, Lea & Febiger.

BARROW, R. (1980) *Happiness,* New York, St Martin's Press.

BARROW, R. (1981) *The Philosophy of Schooling,* Brighton, Harvester Press.

BARROW, R. (1984) *Giving Teaching Back to Teachers,* Brighton, Wheatsheaf.

BEARDSLEY, M.C. (1979) 'In defence of aesthetic value', presidential address at the American Philosophical Association, *Proceedings,* 52, 6.

BECK, L.W. (1959) *Immanuel Kant: Foundations of the Metaphysics of Morals,* Indianapolis, IN, Bobbs-Merrill.

BECK., L.W. (1975) *The Actor and the Spectator,* New Haven, CT, Yale University Press.

BELLAMY, R. (1982) 'Wilander: A winner and a gentleman', *The Times,* 5 June.

BENJAMIN, H. (1971) 'The saber-tooth curriculum' in HOOPER, R. (Ed) *The Curriculum: Context Design and Development,* Edinburgh, Oliver & Boyd, pp.7–19.

BERNDTSON, A. (1960) 'Beauty, embodiment and art', *Philosphy and Phenomenological Research,,* 21.

BEST, D. (1978) *Philosophy and Human Movement,* London, George Allen & Unwin.

BEST, D. (1979) 'Free expression and the teaching of techniques', *British Journal of Educational Studies,* XXVII, 3, October.

BEST, D. (1980) 'The objectivity of artistic appreciation', *British Journal of Aesthetics,* 20, 2, spring, pp.115–27.

BEST, D. (1982) 'Can creativity be taught?', *British Journal of Educational Studies,* 30, 2, October, pp.280–94.

BEST, D. (1985) *Feeling and Reason in the Arts,* London, George Allen & Unwin.

BIGGE, M.C. (1982) *Educational Philosophies for Teachers,* Columbus, OH, Charles E Merrill & Co.

BLOOM, B.S. *et al* (1966) *Taxonomy of Educational Objectives: The Classification of Educational Goals,* London, Longmans.

BLUM, L.A. (1980) *Friendship, Altruism and Morality,* Boston, MA, Routledge & Kegan Paul.

BOROTA, J. (1978) 'A plea for sporting ethics', *Bulletin of the Federation Internationale d'Education Physique,* 48, 3, pp.7–10.

BOUET, M. (1969) *Les Motivations des Sportifs,* Editions Universitaires.

BRISKMAN, L. (1980) 'Creative product and creative process in science and art', *Enquiry,* 23, pp.83–106.

BROOKS, G.H. (Ed) (1981) *Perspectives on the Academic Discipline of Physical Education,* Champaign, IL, Human Kinetic Publishers.

BROWN, S. (1981) *What Do They Know?: A Review of Criterion Referenced Assessment,* London, HMSO.

BUCHER, C.A. (1983) *Foundations of Physical Education and Sport,* St Louis, MI, C.V. Mosby.

BULL, H. (1985) 'The use of behavioural objectives — A moral issue', *Journal of Further and Higher Education,* 9, 3, autumn, pp.74–80.

CALLOIS, R. (1961) *Man, Play and Games,* New York, Free Press of Glencoe.

CARLISLE, R. (1969) 'The concept of physical education', *Proceedings of the Philosophy of Education Society of Great Britain,* 3, January.

CARR. D. (1978) 'Practical pursuits and the curriculum', *Journal of the Philosophy of Education*, 12, pp.69–80.

CARR, D. (1981) 'Knowledge in practice', *American Philosophic Quarterly*, 18, 1, January, pp.53–61.

CARROLL, R. (1982) 'Examination and curriculum change in physical education', *Physical Education Review*, 5, 1, pp.26–36.

CHAPMAN, O.M. (1972) 'Creative dance: Some implications of the concept', *The Laban Art of Movement Guild Magazine*, 49, November, pp.15–19.

COLLINSON, D. (1973) 'Aesthetic education' in LANGFORD, G. and O'CONNOR, D.J. (Eds) *New Essays in the Philosophy of Education*, London, Routledge & Kegan Paul.

CORBIN, C.B and LINDSEY, R. (1984) *Fitness for Life*, Glenview, IL, Scott Foresman and Co.

CRONBACH, L.J. (1963) 'Evaluation for course improvement', *Teacher's College Record*, 64, pp.672–83.

CURL, G.F. (1976) 'The skilful: A major sector of the aesthetic', *Momentum*, 1, 1, spring.

CURL, G.F. (1980) commentary given at a lecture at Dunfermline College, Edinburgh.

CURTIS, B.L. (1977) 'Teaching to and teaching that', *Education Review*, February, pp.83–96.

DAVIS, E.C. (1961) *The Philosophic Process in Physical Education*. Philadelphia, PA, Lea & Febiger.

DAVIES, I.K. (1976) *Objectives in Curriculum Design*, London, McGraw-Hill Company (UK) Ltd.

DEARDEN, R.F. (1968) *The Philsophy of Primary Education*, London, Routledge & Kegan Paul.

DEARDEN, R.F. (1969) 'The concept of play' in PETERS, R.S. (Ed) *The Concept of Education*, London, Routledge & Kegan Paul.

DEARDEN, R.F. (1975) 'Happiness and education' in DEARDEN, R.F., HIRST, P.H. and PETERS, R.S. (Eds) *A Critique of Current Educational Aims*, London, Routledge & Kegan Paul.

DEARDEN, R.F. (1976) *Problems in Primary Education*, London, Routledge & Kegan Paul.

DELATTRE, E.J. (1975) 'Some reflections on success and failure in competitive athletics', *Journal of the Philosophy of Sport*, 2, pp.131–9.

DEWEY, J. (1900) *The School and Society*, Chicago, IL, University of Chicago.

DEWEY, J. (1916) *Democracy and Education*, New York, Macmillan.

DEWEY, J. (1958) *Art as Experience*, New York, Capricorn Books, pp.61–2.

DUNLOP, F. (1975) 'Bailey on games, winning and education', *Cambridge Journal of Education*, 5, 3, Michaelmas, pp.153–60.

DUNLOP, F. (1984) *The Education of Feeling and Emotion*, London, George Allen & Unwin.

EISNER, E.W. (1975) 'Instructional an expressive objectives' in GOLBY, M. GREENWALD, J. and WEST, R. (Eds) *Curriculum Design*, London, Open University Press.

ELLIOTT, R.K. (1971) 'Versions of creativity', *Proceedings of the Philosophy of Education Society*, 5, 2, pp.139–52.

ELLIOTT, R.K. (1972) 'The critic and lover of art' in MAYS, W. and BROWN, S.C. (Eds) *Linguistic Analysis and Phenomenology*, London, Macmillan.

FARSON, R. (1978) 'The technology of humanism', *Journal of Humanistic Psychology*.

FIELDING M. (1976) 'Against competition', *Proceedings of the Philosophy of Education Society of Great Britain*, X, July, pp.124–46.

FISHER, M. (1972) 'Sport as an aesthetic experience' in GERBER, E.W. (Ed) *Sport and the Body*, Philadelphia, PA, Lea & Febiger.

FLIEGLER, L. (1961) 'Dimensions of the creative process' in ANDREWS, M. (Ed) *Creativity and Psychological Health*, Syracuse, NY, Syracuse University.

FOSTER, J. (1971) *Creativity and the Teacher*, London, Macmillan.

FRALEIGH, W.F. (1975) 'Sport-purpose', *Journal of the Philosophy of Sport*, 2, pp.74–82.

FRALEIGH, W.F. (1982) 'Why the good foul is not good enough', *Journal of Physical Education, Recreation and Dance*, 53, January.

FRALEIGH, W.F. (1984) *Right Actions in Sport: Ethics for Contestants*, Champaign, IL, Human Kinetic Publishers.

FREISEN, J. (1975) 'Perceiving dance', *Journal of Aesthetic Education*, 9, 4, October.

GALLIE, W.B. (1955–56) 'Essentially contested concepts', *Proceedings of the Aristotelian Society*, 16, pp.167–98.

GALLIE, W.B. (1964)*Philosophy and Historical Understanding*, London, Chatto & Windus.

GARFORTH, F.W. (1985) *Aims, Values and Education*, Hull, Christygate Press.

GENSEMER, R.E. (1985) *Physical Education: Perspectives, Enquiry Applications*, New York, W.H. Saunders.

GHISELIN, B. (1952)*The Creative Process*, New York, New American Library.

GINGELL J. (1975) 'Perceiving dance', *Journal of Aesthetic Education*, 9, 4, October.

GLASS, G.V. (1978) 'Standards and criteria', *Journal of Educational Measurement*, 15, pp.237–61.

GOODMAN, P. (1971) *Compulsory Miseducation*, Harmondsworth, Penguin.

GRICE, G.R. (1967) *The Grounds of Moral Judgement*, New York, Cambridge University Press, chapter 4.

HARE, R.M. (1981) *Moral Thinking*, New York, Clarendon Press.

HARPER, W. (1977) *The Philosophic Process in Physical Education*, Philadelphia, Lea & Febiger.

HARROW, A.J. (1972) *A Taxonomy of the Psychomotor Domain: A Guide for Developing Behavioural Objectives*, New York, David McKay Company Inc.

HEPBURN, R.W. (1975) 'The arts and the education of feeling and emotion' in DEARDEN, R.F., HIRST, P.H. and PETERS, R.S. (Eds) *Education Reason*, London, Routledge & Kegan Paul.

HERRIGELL, E. (1971) *Zen in the Art of Archery*, New York, Vintage Books.

HIRST, P.H. (1969) 'The logic of the curriculum', *Journal of Curriculum Studies*, 1, p.143.

HIRST, P.H. (1974) *Knowledge and the Curriculum*, London, Routledge & Kegal Paul.

HIRST, P.H. (1979) 'Human movement, knowledge and education', *Journal of the Philosophy of Education*, 13, pp.101–8.

HIRST, P.H. and PETERS, R.S. (1970) *The Logic of Education*, London, Routledge & Kegan Paul.

HOLT, M. (1981) *Evaluating the Evaluators*, London, Hodder & Stoughton.

HOSPERS, J. (1967) *An Introduction to Philosophical Analysis*, London, Routledge & Kegan Paul.

HOSPERS, J. (1985) *Human Conduct: Problems of Ethics*, New York, Harcourt Brace Jovanovich.

HUIZINGA, J. (1970) *Homo Ludens*, London and Boulder, CO, Paladin.

HUXLEY, A. (1969) *Ends and Means: An Enquiry into the Nature of Ideal and into the Methods of Their Realisation*, London, Chatto & Windus.

ILLICH, I. (1973) *Deschooling Society*, Harmondsworth, Penguin.

INTERNATIONAL SKATING UNION (1973–75) *Regulations*.

JEWETT, A.E. and BAIN, L.L. (1985) *The Curriculum Process in Physical Education*, Dubuque, 10, W.C. Brown.

KAELIN, E.F. (1966) *An Existentialist Aesthetic*, London, University of Wisconsin Press.

KAELIN, E.F. (1979) 'The well played game: Towards an aesthetics of sport' in GERBER. E.W. and MORGAN, W.J. (Eds) *Sport and the Body*, Philadelphia, PA, Lea & Febiger.

KANE, J.E. (1974) *Physical Education in Secondary Schools*, London, Schools Council Research Studies, Macmillan.

KANE, J.E. (1976) *Curriculum Development in Physical Education*, London, Crosby, Lockwood, Staples.

KANT, E. (1960) *Education*, translation by Churton, G.A., University of Michigan Press.

KEATING J.W. (1979) 'Sportsmanship as a moral category' in GERBER, E.W. and MORGAN, W.J. (Eds) *Sport and the Body*, 2nd edn, Philadelphia, PA, Lea & Febiger.

KEATING, J.W. (1973) 'The ethics of competition and its relation to moral problems in atheletics' in OSTERHOUDE, R.G. (Ed) *The Philosophy of Sport*, Springfield, IL, Charles Thomas.

KEENAN, F. (1973) 'The athletic contest as a "tragic" form of art' in OSTERHOUDT, R.G. (Ed) *The Philosophy of Sport*, Springfield, IL, Thomas.

KEENAN, F. (1975) 'Justice and sport', *Journal of the Philosophy of Sport*, 2, pp.111–23.

KENYON, G.S. (1968) 'A sociology of sport: On becoming a sub-discipline' in BROWN, R.C. and CRATTY, (Eds) *New Perspectives of Man in Action*. Englewood Cliffs, NJ, Prentice Hall.

KERR, J.F. (1969) *Changing the Curriculum*, London, University of London Press, p.16.

KEW, F.C. (1978) 'Values in competitive games', *Quest*, 29, pp.103–13.

KIRCHNER, G (1985) *Physical Education for Elementary School Children*, Dubuque, 10, W.C. Brown.

KIRK, G. (1986) *The Core Curriculum*, London, Hodder & Stoughton.

KNELLER, G.F. (1967) *The Art and Science of Creativity*, New York, Holt, Rinehart & Winston.

KOHLBERG, L. (1971) 'Stages of moral development as a basis for moral education; in BECK, C.M., CRITTENDEN, B.S. and SULLIVAN, E.S. (Eds) *Moral Education — Interdisciplinary Approaches*, Ontario, University of Toronto Press.

KOLNAI, A. (1965–66) 'Games and aims', *Proceedings of the Aristotelian Society*, pp.103–8.

KRATWOHL, D.R. *et al* (1956) *Taxonomy of Educational Objectives: Handbook II: The Affective Domain*, New York, David McKay Company Inc.

LABAN, R. (1963) *Modern Educational Dance*, 2nd edn, revised by ULLMAN, L. New York, Frederick A Praeger.

LANGFORD, G.(1968) *Philosophy and Education*, London, Macmillan.

LARSON, L.A. (1976) *Foundations of Physical Activity*, New York, Macmillan.

LAWTON, D. (1973) *Social Change, Educational Theory and Curriculum Planning*, London, University of London Press.

LAWTON, D. (1980) *The Politics of the School Curriculum*, London, Routledge & Kegan Paul.

LEHMAN, C. (1981) 'Can cheaters play the game?' *Journal of the Philosophy of Sport*, 7, pp.41–6.

LOGSDON, B.J. *et al* (1984) *Physical Education for Children*, Philadelphia, PA, Lea and Febiger.

LOWE, B. (1977) *The Beauty of Sport*, New York, Prentice Hall.

LUCAS, J.R. (1959) 'Moralists and gamesmen', *Philosophy*, 34, II, pp.1–11.

LUFF, I.V. (1980) 'Curriculum evaluation: A neglected process', *Physical Education Review*, 3, 1.

LYONS, N.P. (1983) 'Two perspectives: On self, relationships and morality', *Harvard Educational Review*, 53, May, pp.125–45.

MCINTOSH, P. (1979) *Fair Play: Ethics in Sport and Education*, London, Heinemann.

MCINTYRE, A. (1971) *Against the Self Images of the Age*, London, Duckworth.

MACLURE, S. (1983) 'Growing up in the eighties', *Times Educational Supplement*, 26 August, p.2.

MAGER, R.F. (1962) *Preparing Instructional Objectives*, Belmont-Feuson, p.13.

MAHEU, R. (1962) 'Sport and culture', *International Journal of Adult and Youth Education*, 14, 4.

MARAJ, J.A. (1965) 'Physical education and character', *Education Review*, 17, 2, February.

MARTIN, J.R. (1981) 'Needed: A new paradigm for liberal education' in SOLTIS, J.F. (Ed) *Philosophy and Education, 80th Year Book, NSEE*, Chicago, IL, University of Chicago Press.

MEAKIN, D.C. (1981) 'Physical education: An agency of moral education?' *Journal of the Philosophy of Education*, 15, 2, pp.241–53.

MEAKIN, D.C. (1982) 'Moral values and physical education', *Physical Education Review*, 5, 1, pp.62–82.

MEAKIN, D.C. (1983) 'On the justification of physical education', *Momentum*, 8, 3, autumn, pp.10–18.

MEAKIN, D.C. (1986) 'The moral status of competition', *Journal of the Philosophy of Education*, 20, 1, pp.59–67.

MERLEAU-PONTY, M. (1949) *La Structure du Comportement,* Paris, Presses Universitaires de Paris.

METHENY, E. (1965) *Connotations of Movement in Sport and Dance,* Dubuque, IO, Brown.

MIDGLEY, M. (1974) 'The game game', *Philosophy,* 49, pp.231–53.

MORRIS, S. (Ed) (1979) *The Book of Strange Facts and Useless Information,* New York, Dolskin.

MORRISON, R. (1969) *A Movement Approach to Educational Gymnastics,* London, J.M. Dent & Son.

NICKLAUS, J. (1974) *Golf My Way,* New York, Simon & Schuster.

NISBET, S. (1972) *Purpose in the Curriculum,* London, University of London Press.

NIXON, J.E. and JEWETT, A.E. (1980) *An Introduction to Physical Education,* Saunders College, Philadelphia, PA, Holt, Rinehart & Winston.

NORTH, M. (1973) *Movement Education,* London, Temple Smith.

OAKESHOTT, M. (1962) *Rationalism in Politics,* London, Methuen.

O'HEAR, A. (1981) *Education, Society and Human Nature,* London, Routledge & Kegan Paul.

OLDFIELD, R.S. (1959) 'The analysis of human skill' in HALMOS, P. and ILIFFE, A. (Eds) *Readings in General Psychology,* London, Routledge & Kegan Paul.

OLFORD, J.E. (1971) 'The concept of creativity', *Proceedings of the Philosophy of Education Society,* 5, pp.77–95.

Open University (1972) *Curriculum Philosophy and Design,* course E283, units 6–8.

Open University (1976) *Rationality and Artistry,* course E203, units 16–18.

OZMAN, H.A. and CRAVER, S.M. (1981) *Philosophical Foundations of Education,* Columbus, OH, Bell & Howell.

PARLETT, M. and HAMILTON, D. (1975) 'Evaluation as illumination' in TAWNEY, D. (Ed) *Curriculum Evaluation Today: Trends and Implications,* London, Schools Council Research Studies, Macmillan.

PERRY, L.R. (1975) 'Competition and cooperation', *British Journal of Educational Studies,* XXIII, 2, June.

PETERS, R.S. (1963) *Authority, Responsibility and Education,* London, Allen & Unwin.

PETERS, R.S. (1966) *Ethics and Education,* London, George Allen & Unwin.

PETERS, R.S. (1973a) 'Aims of education' in PETERS, R.S. (Eds) *The Philosophy of Education,* London, Oxford University Press, pp.11–29.

PETERS, R.S. (1973b) 'The justification of education' in PETERS, R.S. (Ed) *The Philosophy of Education,* London, Oxford University Press, pp.239–67.

PETERS, R.S (1975) 'The education of the emotions' in DEARDEN, R.F., HIRST, P.H. and PETERS, R.S. *Education and Reason,* London, Routledge & Kegan Paul.

PETERS, R.S. (1981a) 'Moral education and the psychology of character' in PETERS, R.S. (Ed) *Moral Development and Moral Education,* London, George Allen & Unwin.

PETERS, R.S. (1981b) 'Democratic values and educational aims' in PETERS, R.S. (Ed) *Essays on Educators,* London, George Allen & Unwin.

PHENIX, P.H. (1970) 'Relationship in dance to other art forms' in HABERMAN,

M. and MEISEL, T.G. (Eds) *Dance an Art in Academe,* New York, Teachers College Press.

PLATO (1955) *The Republic,* translation by LEE, H.D.P., Harmondsworth, Penguin.

POLANYI, M. (1973) *Personal Knowledge,* London, Routledge & Kegan Paul.

POPHAM, W.J. *et al* (1969) *Instructional Objectives,* Chicago, IL, American Educational Research Association monograph series on 'Curriculum Evaluation', 3.

PRING, R. (1976) *Knowledge and Schooling,* London, Open Books.

PRING, R. (1981) 'Monitoring performance: Reflections on the Assessment of Performance Unit' in LACEY, C. and LAWTON, D. (Eds) *Issues in Evaluation and Accountability,* London, Methuen, pp.156–88.

PRING, R. (1984) *Personal and Social Education in the Curriculum,* London, Hodder & Stoughton.

PRVULOVICH, Z.R. (1982) 'In defense of competition', *Journal of the Philosophy of Education,* 16, 1, pp.77–88.

RAWLS, J. (1958) 'Justice as fairness', *The Philosophy Review,* LXVII, 2, April.

RAWLS, J. (1972) *A Theory of Justice,* Oxford, Oxford University Press.

REDFERN, H.B. (1983) *Dance, Art and Aesthetics,* London, Dance Books Limited.

REDFERN, H.B. (1984) *Concepts in Modern Educational Dance,* London, Kimpton.

REDFERN, H.B. (1986) *Questions in Aesthetic Education,* London, Allen & Unwin.

REID, L.A. (1961) *Ways of Knowledge and Experience,* London, Allen & Unwin.

REID, L.A. (1979) 'Knowledge, aesthetic insight and education', *Proceedings of the Philosophy of Education Society of Great Britain,* 7, 1, pp.66–84.

REID, L.A. (1986) *Ways of Understanding and Education,* London, Heinemann.

REIMER, B. (1970) *A Philosophy of Music Education,* New York, Prentice Hall.

REIMER, E. (1971) *School is Dead,* New York, Doubleday.

RIVENES, R.S. (1978) *Foundations of Physical Education,* Boston OMA, Houghton Mifflin.

RYLE, G. (1949) *The Concept of Mind,* Oxford, Blackwell.

RYLE, G. (1975) 'Can virtue be taught?' in DEARDEN, R.F., HIRST, P.H. and PETERS, R.S. (Eds) *Education and Reason,* London, Routledge & Kegan Paul.

SAGE, G. (1984) *Motor Learning and Control,* Dubuque, IO, W.C. Brown.

SALVAN, J. (1966) *To Be and Not To Be,* Wayne State University Press.

SATTERLY, D. (1981) *Assessment in Schools,* Oxford, Blackwell.

SCHILLING, M. (1986) 'Knowledge and liberal education: A critique of Paul Hirst', *Journal of Curriculum Studies,* 18, 1, pp.1–16.

SCHMITZ, K.L. (1979) 'Sport and play: Suspension of the ordinary' in GERBER, E.W. and MARGAN, W.J. (Eds) *Sport and the Body,* 2nd edn, Philadelphia, PA, Lea & Febiger.

Schools Council (1982) *Examinations in Physical Education and Related Areas,* London, Schools Council.

SCOTT, J. (1973) 'Sport and the radical ethic', *Quest,* 19, January, pp.71–7.

Scottish Central Committee on Physical Education (1985) *A Framework for*

Assessment, an occasional paper, Edinburgh, Scottish Central Committee on Physical Education, August.

Scottish Committee on Expressive Arts in the Primary School (1983) *Towards a Policy for expressive Arts in the Primary School,* Edinburgh, Scottish Committee on Expressive Arts in the Primary School.'

Scottish Education Department (1977) *The Structure of the Curriculum* (The Munn Report), Edinburgh, HMSO.

SHEA, E.J. (1978) *Ethical Decisions in Physical Education and Sport,* Springfield, IL, C. Thomas.

SIMON, R.L. (1985) *Sports and Social Values,* Englewood Cliffs, NJ. Prentice Hall.

SIMONS, H. (1981) 'Process accountability in schools' in LACEY, C. and LAWTON, D. (Eds) *Issues in Evaluation and Accountability,* London, Methuen, pp.114–44.

SINGER, R.H. (1980) *Motor Learning and Human Performance,* New York, Macmillan.

SKILBECK, M. (1980) *Evaluating the Curriculum in the 80s,* London, Hodder & Stoughton.

SLUSHER, H. (1967) *Man, Sport and Existence,* Philadelphia, PA, Lea & Febiger.

SOCKETT, H. (1976) *Designing the Curriculum,* London, Open Books.

SOCKETT, H. (1979) 'The concept of curriculum innovation' in Open University *Curriculum Evaluation,* units 19, 20 and 21 of course E203 on 'Curriculum design and development', Milton Keynes, Open University Press.

SOCKETT, H. (1980) *Accountability in the English Education System,* London, Hodder & Stoughton.

STENHOUSE, L. (1970–71) 'Some limitations of the use of objectives in curriculum research and planning', *Paedagogica Europa,* 6.

STENHOUSE, L. (1978) *An Introduction to Curriculum Research and Development,* London, Heinemann.

STOLNITZ, J. (1960) *Aesthetics and Philosophy of Art Criticism,* Houghton Mifflin.

STOLNITZ, J. (1973) 'The artistic values in aesthetic experience', *Journal of Aesthetic and Art Criticism,* 32, 1.

STRAUGHAN, R. and WRIGLEY, J. (Eds) (1980) *Values and Evaluation in Education,* London, Harper & Row.

STRAWSON, P.F. (1967) 'Aesthetic appraisal and works of art', *Oxford Review,* pp.5–13.

TABA, H. (1962) *Curriculum Development,* New York, Harcourt Brace & World.

THOMPSON, K. (1975) 'The point of an activity', *Cambridge Journal of Education,* 5, 3, Michaelmas.

THOMPSON, K. (1983) 'The justification of physical education', *Momentum,* 8, 2, autumn, pp.19–23

TYLER, R.W. (1971) *Basic Principles of Curriculum and Instruction,* Chicago, IL, University of Chicago Press.

URMSON, J.O. (1958) 'Saints and heroes' in MELDEN, A.I. (Ed) *Essays in Moral Philosophy,* Seattle, WA, University of Washington Press.

VERNON, P.E. (Ed) (1972) *Creativity,* London, Penguin Books

WALLAS, G. (1926) *The Art of Thought,* New York, Harcourt Brace & World.

WALLER, D. and GILROY, A. (1978) *Ideas in Art Therapy,* London, British Association of Art Therapy.

WARNOCK, M. (1977) *Schools of Thought,* London, Faber & Faber.

WEITZ, M. (1970) 'The role of theory in aesthetics' in WEITZ, M. (Ed) *Problems in Aesthetics,* 2nd edn, Toronto, Macmillan.

WHITE, J. (1971) 'The concept of curriculum evaluation', *Journal of Curriculum Studies,* 3, 2, November.

WHITE, J.P. (1973) *Towards a Compulsory Curriculum,* London, Routledge & Kegan Paul.

WHITE, J.P. (1975) Creativity and education: A philosophical analysis' in DEARDEN, R.F., HIRST, P.H. and PETERS, R.S. (Eds) *A Critique of Current Educational Aims,* London, Routledge & Kegan Paul.

WHITE, J.P. (1982) *The Aims of Education Restated,* London, Routledge & Kegan Paul.

WHITE, J.R. (Ed) (1966) 'Gymnastics', *Sports Rules Encyclopaedia,* pp.293–4.

WILLIAMS, B. (1976) 'Persons, character and morality' in RORTY, A.O. (Ed) *The Identity of Persons,* Berkeley, CA, University of California Press.

WILLIAMS, N. (1981) 'An eclectic approach to evaluation' in LACEY, C. and LAWTON, D. (Eds) *Issues in Evaluation and Accountability,* London, Methuen.

WILSON, J. (1970) *Moral Thinking,* London, Heinemann.

WILSON, J., WILLIAMS, N. and SUGARMAN, B. (1967) *Introduction to Moral Education,* Harmondsworth, Penguin.

WILSON, P. (1980) 'Aesthetic education and the compulsory curriculum', *Journal of Curriculum Studies,* 12, 1, pp.29–39.

WITTGENSTEIN, L. (1953) *Philosophical Investigations,* Oxford, Blackwell.

WRIGHT, D. (1971) *The Psychology of Moral Behaviour,* Harmondsworth, Penguin.

ZEIGLER, E.F. (1964) *Philosophical Foundations for Physical, Health and Recreation Education,* Englewood, Cliffs, NJ, Prentice Hall.

ZEIGLER, E.F. (1978) *An Introduction to the Philosophy of Physical Education and Sport,* Champaign, IL, Stipes Publishing Co.

Author Index

Subject Index

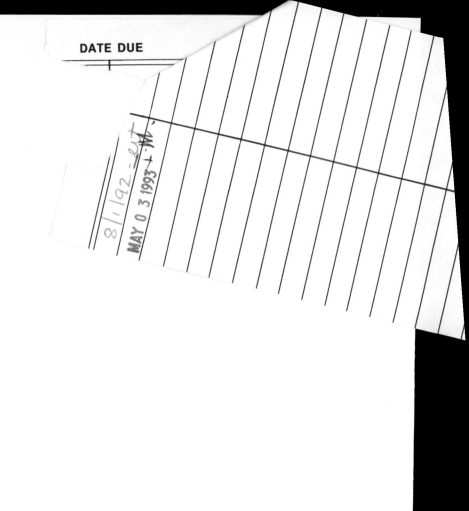